Shad Helmstetter, Ph.D.

WHO
Are You
Really
And What
Do You
WANT?

PARK
AVENUE
PRESS
www.ParkAvenuePress.com

Books by Shad Helmstetter:

What To Say When You Talk To Your Self
The Self-Talk Solution
Choices
Predictive Parenting
Finding The Fountain of Youth Inside Yourself
You Can Excel in Times of Change
Self-Talk for Weight-Loss
Network of Champions
American Victory
Fired Up!
Goals-On-Line.com

Who Are You Really And What Do You Want?

Helmstetter, Shad
    Who Are You Really And What Do You Want?

ISBN 0-9727821-0-9

Printed in USA

10 9 8 7 6 5 4 3

This book is dedicated in loving memory of my mother,
Nora Anna Helmstetter

Who Are You *Really* And What Do You Want?

by Shad Helmstetter, Ph.D.

Table of Contents

Chapter One

The Best of the Best

This book should be an exciting book for you. I hope it is. This book is about *you*—the *real* you—and the very real goal of getting what you really want out of your life.

My personal goal for this book is to give you the tools to help take some of the "self" out of "self-help," so you have the support you need to truly succeed. I intend to present to you the best of what we've learned in the past three decades of personal growth, in a dynamic three-part process that is literally re-shaping the world of self-help today.

In these pages I'm going to give you a systematic solution to self-help and personal achievement that is so practical, and so rewarding, that I think you'll agree it is an exceptional solution for getting better—in virtually *any* area of your life.

This is a solution anyone can use. It works whether you want to lose weight, increase your income, work on an important relationship, change a habit, get your career on track, or improve yourself in some other way.

The solution works because it brings together, for the first time in any book of this kind, three fundamental principles that are *essential* to positive change—the three ingredients that make the best self-help concepts *work!*

The three-part discovery I'm sharing with you here began with my own journey through the world of personal growth many years ago, and my lifelong goal to help people do better—to live up to the *promise* of their true potential.

Because of that goal, I've spent most of my adult life working in the field of personal growth. Over the past thirty years I have researched and explored literally every form of self-help—some that lasted, and many that did not.

My objective all along has been to find the *real* solutions to self-improvement—to separate the practical from the not-so-practical, and find out what works for real people. This book is the result.

As I prepared to write this book, I found myself taking a look at where my own search began so many years ago with the process of life coaching—a form of personal coaching that helps people get better and move forward in important areas of their lives.

HELPING PEOPLE FIND THE ANSWERS

I first began coaching people in the early 1970s, at a time

when the benefits of personal coaching had not yet been fully discovered. I had developed an approach that I believed would help anyone who went through a specific coaching process which I called *Who Are You and What Do You Want?*

I had decided right from the start that my role as a coach would *not* be that of an advisor or counselor. I believed strongly even then, as I do now, that coaching should *not* be a form of therapy or psychological counseling. Coaching, instead, should help people find direction, stay motivated, and move forward.

I decided I would guide my clients, but I would guide them with *questions*. I suspected that each of them already had the right answers within them—they just hadn't found them yet. No one had ever asked them the right questions to help them figure it out.

My approach to coaching was simple and straightforward, but it worked—exceptionally well. Instead of giving personal advice or offering clients *my* opinion, I learned to ask the right questions. In so doing, I helped them help themselves by identifying their *focus* and *plan of action* while I remained objective and supportive.

THE FIRST BREAKTHROUGH

After personally guiding dozens of people through this early process of personal coaching, I observed that in *every* case, all of them had begun to figure out who they actually were, *inside*; to identify specifically what they wanted; and determine what they had to do next.

That coaching program was my first step toward finding the answers to helping people get better. Over time, the coaching program continued to prove to be successful; I saw my clients make changes that would affect their lives in positive ways for years to come.

It was years before even the terms "life coach" or "personal coach" (or "business coach") would be invented— but the success of that early coaching program showed me that regular people could make incredible progress when they had the right direction and support.

And the experience led to my first of the three breakthrough concepts in the world of personal growth that I'm going to share with you in this book:

Breakthrough #1: *Personal Coaching*

All self-help works better, when you have help. If you want to do your best, get the right help.

Now, after three decades of seeing coaching first begin to grow, and then come into its own as a respected force in the field of personal growth, although I no longer conduct private coaching sessions myself, I continue my research into the life-changing world of coaching. I also continue to write and share the best ideas I've found for effective coaching with people all over the world. The book you're reading right now is an example of that.

Another coaching format I've undertaken for a number of years is the *"Personal Life Coach Letter,"* which I write and E-mail every week or two in a personalized format to nearly

4

a hundred thousand individuals throughout the world.

To make it possible for other individuals to do what I do—help people get better—I've also trained other people to become professional coaches, teaching them specific coaching methods that I developed as a result of my research and experience in the field.

I mention this history so you'll know that when I'm talking to you in these pages, you can be confident of getting the right message and the right support—the kind a good coach might give you—and you'll know what's behind it.

When it comes to finding the answers to the #1 coaching question of all, *"Who are you, really—and what do you want?"* I've been there before, many times, helping individuals just like you discover the answer to that all-important question for themselves.

OPENING THE DOOR
TO THE NEXT DISCOVERY

We'll examine the idea of personal coaching in greater detail later on in the book, but since the journey to this three-part solution began with the breakthrough of personal coaching, I wanted to familiarize you with the concept right up front.

Personal coaches today are people who are trained to help you find the right focus, identify what you want, and determine what to do next—and they keep you on track and keep you motivated along the way.

As we go through this book together, I'll be helping you

in some ways like a live coach would help, including asking you some of the same kinds of questions that good coaches ask. I think you'll find your answers will be revealing and enlightening—and most of all, *useful*.

I recognized early on that helping people through personal coaching was one of the keys I'd been looking for. I had no idea then how true that would turn out to be. It was my first experience coaching others, along with years and years of real-life results, that proved to me that people actually *could* make positive and lasting changes in their lives—if they could just find a way to get *themselves* out of the way.

As it turned out, I had discovered the first key element to what would become the three-part system contained in this book. But it would take many more years of work and two more major discoveries before I would put it all together.

THE SECOND BREAKTHROUGH

A primary question that kept coming back to me in my coaching and in my research was "Why are some people successful in life, while others are not? What is the real difference between them?" That recurring question led me to the research that would become my first book, *What to Say When You Talk to Your Self.*

In that book, which went on to find a worldwide audience, I presented the findings that proved all of us, and our successes in life, are the result of our mental "programs"—the messages we received and were unconsciously programmed with, especially while we were growing up. I used the term "Self-Talk" to identify the process of changing our programs.

I learned that a key difference between those who succeed and those who don't is the difference in the *programs* they received.

The recognition that all of our successes and failures are tied to our programming proved to be a profound and life-changing discovery. It was the next breakthrough:

Breakthrough #2: Self-Talk

Change your Self-Talk and you will change your programs. Change your programs and you will change your life.

As I wrote a number of books that followed *What to Say When You Talk to Your Self*, I explored the most important aspects of motivational behavior and looked for every possible answer to the question, *"What puts us into motion, and what stops us?"*

It was during this time that I discovered the third break-through; it was something that had been with me the entire time.

THE FINAL INGREDIENT

Even before I had committed to making a serious study of self-improvement, I had begun setting goals for myself.

Later, as I began writing, I continued to set goals in my personal life, in my work, and especially in important areas such as publishing deadlines.

When my publishers expected a completed book manuscript from me, they expected it to be on time. (How difficult or how easy the writing was made no difference to them.) And it was only through setting very specific goals—often daily and weekly goals—that I was able to turn in each of my manuscripts on time.

But it was a chance encounter with an old stack of "goal cards" that caused me to take a whole new look at goal-setting.

Years earlier I had written down my goals on 5x8 index cards. In doing this, I had developed a very precise, but simple, process. I would define each goal and outline my goal plan—exactly what I had to do to reach that goal. Then I would review my goal cards on a regular basis to track my progress.

Five years had gone by when one day, by chance, I found one of my old sets of goal cards in a forgotten file, and I sat down for a moment to read through them. What I found was astonishing! Card after card, goal after goal, every goal I had written down, years earlier, as if by magic—I had achieved!

I had even reached the goals I had thought were impossible when I wrote them down. On one of my blue index cards I had written the goal *"To write a best-selling book that will help people, become a million-seller, and be published worldwide."*

Although I'd written that goal when I didn't have the slightest idea how to go about writing a book like that, or even if it could be done—and many of my friends told me I'd never do it—that book is now in print in 65 countries around the world. I still have the original blue goal card on which I wrote that "impossible" goal.

It was as though, on those few index cards, I had written the script for the screenplay of the coming years of my own life—and all of it had come true! (In a later chapter, I'll share with you the actual goal-setting process that helped me do that.)

Yet, my research had shown me that many other goal-setting systems failed, or they worked for a time, and then stopped working. In fact, I was disappointed to find so much written about goals that appeared to be completely inaccurate! I decided to dig deeper and find out *which* goal-setting techniques actually *worked*—and *why*.

What I suspected turned out to be true: good goal-setting always follows *specific* steps and rules. And most of the goal-setting rules we were taught were the *wrong* rules. When people either didn't know the real rules of goal-setting, or when they followed the wrong rules, most of them failed to reach their goals, and in time, they gave up.

That discovery led to the third breakthrough:

Breakthrough #3: <u>Active *Goal-Setting*</u>

Successful goal-setting follows specific steps. If you want your goals to work, they have to be set and tracked in the right way.

Each of those three foundational concepts, by themselves —Self-Talk, *Active* Goal-Setting, and Personal Coaching—has been used by people to make positive changes in their lives. A close review of the field of personal growth will tell you that all three of those "breakthroughs" are actually seminal concepts for creating true and lasting change. I happened upon them and recognized them for what they were only because I went looking for them.

But while various self-help authors had touched on one or another of these concepts in the past, no one had explored them in depth, and no one had put all three of them *together*. Doing that, *putting them together*, proved to be the key.

PUTTING THEM ALL TOGETHER

By this time, I was devoting much of my schedule to being interviewed on radio and television programs throughout the United States and speaking to live audiences all over the world. As time went on, I focused on the key topics of *Self-Talk, Active Goal-Setting*, and *Personal Coaching*, what I knew by then to be the three most important foundation stones to personal growth—whether someone's goal was building a business, or having a better marriage, or having more money in the bank—*anything* at all.

But as I answered the frequently-asked question about which of those three self-help solutions was ultimately the best, I began to study what would happen if all *three* of the essential self-help ingredients—*Self-Talk reprogramming, the right goal-setting techniques*, and *coaching support*—were brought *together* as one practical, but all-encompassing approach to personal growth.

What if you used all three breakthroughs *at the same time?* What if you started by getting the right *programs*, learned how to set the right *goals* in precisely the right way, and had the right kind of *coaching and encouragement* at the same time? It was clear—*that* combination would almost *guarantee* success!

For the past several years, my work has focused on bringing these three solutions together. What I had predicted proved to be true: individually, each of the three concepts is exceptional; *together*, they are incredible!

THREE ESSENTIAL TOOLS

I've always been against the idea of applying clever names to good self-help ideas. Most self-help ideas that get popular names attached to them tend to fall *out* of popularity just as quickly as they fell *in*, and in a few years, no matter how good they were, or how many people they helped, the ideas end up being relegated to the unread pages of forgotten books, sitting in silence on dusty shelves. There are almost no exceptions to that rule.

The ideas I'm presenting to you here are not a passing fad. The ideas themselves were here long before I wrote about them, and they will be just as true at any time in the future. But in my experience in the field of self-improvement, I've come to learn that these three concepts are so important that they ought to be included as part of the *foundation* of *any* program of personal or professional growth.

In these pages, I'll be showing you how to put these three concepts to work in your own life, by using them for what they are: three essential *tools*, which, when used *together*, can help you achieve almost anything you want to accomplish.

THE BENEFITS ARE YOURS TO KEEP

This, then, is the solution to self-help I now share with the people I care about most—people all over the world. I've also taught this three-part system of personal growth to other individuals who, as successful professional coaches themselves, are now helping even more people succeed. They're helping people make positive steps forward in their lives, because they're using *all three* of these personal growth tools instead of focusing on just one or two of them.

That's exactly what we're going to do together in the short time it takes for you to read this book—and the benefits will be yours to keep for a lifetime.

First, we're going to look at your *self*—and your *Self-Talk*—so you can discover more of who you really are, and how to bring that person to life.

Next, I'm going to show you how, with *active* goal-setting, to identify and set your *goals* in the right way—and discover what you *really* want—not just the big lifelong goals, but the goals that help you do better each and every day. I'm going to help you get goal-setting right.

And finally, I'm going to show you how you can get the right *coaching*—the right support—so you'll find your focus, stay on track, and have the help, encouragement, and motivation you need along the way.

One of the things I found again and again as I studied self-help concepts is, *"if it isn't simple, it will not last."* You'll find that the solution I share with you here is simple. It makes incredible sense; it works—and it *lasts*.

IT'S TIME FOR *YOU!*

What I'm sharing with you here is the best of what I've learned from all of my years of looking for ways to help us get better. This is the best of the *best*.

We'll take each of the three breakthroughs one at a time, and cover each of them in detail. Along the way, I'll make suggestions and provide specific techniques you can apply *now*, even while you're reading the book.

Let's begin by taking a more in-depth look at the first key element. Let's get started with *you*—and your *Self-Talk!*

PART ONE

Your Self-Talk & Your Programs

"Change your Self-Talk
and you will change
your programs.

Change your programs
and you will change
your life."

Chapter Two

Your *Self* and Your *Self-Talk*

To help you understand who you are, and how you can reach *your* goals, it will help to know how the success mechanism that guides us really works.

There is a *reason* some people are successful in their lives—and other people are not. It has to do with their *programming*. Here's how it works:

Like a powerful personal computer, your brain is designed to store—and *act* on—the programs you receive.

From the moment you were born, every message you've ever received has been recorded, chemically and electrically, in neural pathways in your brain. Everything you've ever heard, seen, said, or done has been stored—permanently—in your mental computer. Every message you received from your parents, your brothers or sisters, your friends, your teachers at school, television, the world around you . . . *every* message you received was programmed into your brain.

In many ways your brain *is* like a super-computer. There are differences, of course, but like a computer, your brain stores the messages that get programmed into it—and then it *acts* on the input it has received.

Imagine that if when each of us arrived on Earth as a newborn baby, there was a small computer keyboard strapped to our little chest. Unfortunately, at some point during the excitement of our arrival, the sign got knocked off the top of our keyboard—the sign that used to read:

WARNING . . .
EVERYTHING YOU TYPE INTO THIS CHILD'S
MENTAL COMPUTER WILL BE STORED FOR
LIFE—AND ACTED ON AS THOUGH IT'S TRUE!

Instead of arriving armed with that all-important instruction that should have been given right away to our new programmers (our parents, siblings, teachers, friends at school and finally, to each of *us*), we came with no instructional guidelines for how to program the wonderful mechanism called the human brain. It is as if we helplessly held our little keyboards out to the world, all unsuspecting and innocent, and said,

"Here, Mom . . . here, Dad . . . here, world . . . tell me who I am! Tell me how high I can climb and how far I can go and how much I can do with the unlimited potential in front of me. Type in for me (since I can't yet do it for myself) the picture of me I'm going to become."

Our parents and teachers and friends did the best they

16

could—but *they* didn't know what *we* now know about how we get programmed from birth.

THE TRUTH ABOUT PROGRAMMING

A curious, but important, fact of the human brain is that it is designed to accept *whatever we put into it*—whether what we put into it is *true* or *not!* The brain, like a giant computer storage center, is designed to take in whatever we give it, whether it's true, false, good, bad, right, wrong, positive, or negative. Whatever is "typed" into our computer key-board—our five senses—our brain stores permanently. And what it is told most, it automatically accepts as *truth*:

> *"Suzie, you're going to grow up to be chubby, just like your Aunt Harriet!"*
> *"Tommy, you never tell the truth. I can never believe a thing you say."*
> *"Jason is Mommy's little chatterbox."*
> *"Christy, you're so clumsy. You'll never be a ballerina."*
> *"Kevin, you're going to sleep your entire life away!"*
> *"Thomas Edward, you're just like your father. You'll never amount to anything!"*
> *"Sometimes I wish you had never been born!"*
> *"Audrey, can't you do anything right?"*
> *"Cheryl, you don't care a thing about your grades. You never have and you never will."*
> *"Ricky? You, president? That'll be the day."*

Our *conscious* mind might not accept those kinds of programs—at least not at first—but the storage center of our brain is taking them in, just the same. In time, how we see ourselves, what we think, what we believe, and what we accept as the truth, are all the result of the programs we got. That means *all* of those messages you and I got when we were growing up are actually *programs* that are still *there*, and we're still living with them today.

But it goes beyond that. Behavioral researchers have told us that during the first 18 years of our lives, if we grew up in reasonably positive homes, you and I were told *"No!"* or what we *could not* do, more than 148,000 times!

I happen to believe that's a low estimate. A lot of the messages we got weren't even spoken out loud—you know, like that *look* we got at the dinner table when company had come over. Or the parent who didn't show up for some event that he or she should have attended. We all got messages, spoken and unspoken—tens of thousands of them—and all too many of them were the wrong kind.

GETTING THE MESSAGE, AGAIN AND AGAIN

But whether it was a hundred times we were told what we were *not* good at, or that we weren't smart enough or strong enough . . . or many times more than that, we eventually got the message. We didn't even have to know we had gotten it. Our computer brains don't have a special warning *"beep"*

18

that goes off every time a negative message comes in. Our brain just programs it in and goes on about its business. Message after message . . . day after day . . . year after year.

Of course, and we can be thankful for this, not all of the messages we got were bad. Some of them were good. But with most of us, the truth is that when it came to being born as brilliant sparks of creation, ready to light up our lives with the fire of exceptional achievement, we got more messages that *diminished* us than those that breathed life into the fire of our own potential. (I know some people whose fires went out before they even got out of school, and they never figured out how to light them again.)

The people around us didn't *try* to give us the wrong programs, of course. *They were just handing down to us the programs they had gotten themselves.*

THE PROGRAMS WE GOT *THEN* CREATE THE SELF-TALK WE HAVE *NOW*

The programming we got as children was just the beginning. While we continued blissfully unaware along our way, we continued to get programmed by every possible input around us.

Never mind that we didn't *ask* the people in the world around us to give us their programs—their opinions—they happily gave them to us anyway. They somehow thought it was their right to project their negative programs onto our potentially promising path. Even as adults we are surrounded by people who think it is their responsibility to share their questionable programs with us.

(Obviously, our Creator intended that the people who programmed us would love us, want to nurture us, figure out what they were doing, and get it right. Unfortunately, there are people in this world who didn't get it right.)

Meanwhile, as we got older, our own computers clicked in, and we ourselves began to *duplicate* and *repeat* the same kinds of programs that we had gotten from the world around us—and *we* became our own #1 programmers.

REPEATING THE MESSAGES
FOR OURSELVES

The way the programming process works in the human brain, we automatically *duplicate and repeat* the strongest of the programs we received from everyone else. Although many of the hundreds of thousands of programs we got from the rest of the world were exactly the *wrong* programs, we began to repeat those same programs as our *own*. Our own self-talk became a *reflection* of the strongest programs we already carried within us.

So those programs, that we duplicated and repeated, thought after thought, day after day, got stronger and stronger the more we repeated them. (To do this, all you have to do is think the same thought again, or see the same picture again in your mind—or even feel the same emotions again—and *"click,"* you've just added another program to the file.) Every time they're repeated, the old programs get stronger, until they become an automatic and unconscious part of *what* we think and *how* we think.

The result is a litany of sclf-talk which is often negative, and all too familiar. When I wrote the book *What to Say When You Talk to Your Self*, I included a list of one hundred of the most negative self-talk phrases people use without even thinking about it. For example:

Nothing ever goes right for me.
Some people have all the luck.
Everything I eat goes right to my waist.
I'm just no good at that.
I get sick this same time every year.
Why me?
I'm so stupid!
Another blue Monday.
I've tried to lose weight, but nothing works for me.
Nobody likes me.
I can't remember names.
I'm just not creative.
I never have enough time.
My desk is always a mess.
Sometimes I just hate myself.
I'm too shy.
I never know what to say.
I can never afford the things I want.
I'm such a wimp!
I'll be lucky if I . . .
I'm not proud.
I can't do anything about it—it's just the way I am.

I just can't seem to make ends meet.
Why even bother?
It's just not my day . . .
. . . and on, and on, and on.

Are those really the kinds of self-directions that fill our computers and manage our minds? Unfortunately, *yes*, they are.

It's not that some of those things we say about ourselves aren't *true*—by now, most of them probably are. But what do you suppose *made* them that way? Also unsettling is the recognition that for every one of those kinds of rather minor expressions we hear ourselves say, there are thousands of other programs, just as negative, hiding beneath the surface. It is those hidden programs that are often the strongest of all. These are the programs that determine our *self-esteem*, our *self-confidence*, our *attitudes*, our *beliefs*, and most of our *actions*.

The result is that the sum total of our programs, whatever they are, *positive*, *negative*, or *neutral*, influences or controls almost everything about us. When we recognize the impact of that in our lives, we begin to understand the answer to the question, *"Why are some people successful, and some people are not?"*

Researchers have told us that as much as *77%* of the programs we carry with us are negative, counter-productive, or work against us! Not everyone is that bad off, of course— but then, look around you. I know people who are failing so completely in their lives that it looks as though nearly *all* of their programs are the *wrong* programs.

In every case, when you study a person carefully, you will

always find that the person's *success* or *failure* is ultimately the result of that individual's *programs*.

A WALK THROUGH "SELF-TALK PARK"

What we're talking about here is not theory; it is medical, neurological, scientific fact. Today, with the help of medical computer imaging technology, we can even watch the programming process at work, in the neuron structure of the brain, *while* it's happening. Without going into a seminar on the brain, I'll simplify the process and show you how it works. To do that, I'd like you to imagine that you're taking a walk through a place I'll call "Self-Talk Park."

The park you're visiting is quite large, and between the widely-spaced trees it's covered with lush, green grass. When you first see the park, there are no paths there yet; no one has walked there before. The first time you walk through the park, you notice that even though you're walking through the grass, you're not leaving much of a trail. You've only passed by that way once. The next time you visit the park and walk through it, you follow the same route again. But still you don't leave much of a trail.

However, as you begin to visit the park more often, each time following the same route, you start to notice you can now see a slight trail—the beginning of a pathway. Later, each time you walk through Self-Talk Park, you will *automatically* follow your new pathway. And now, today, because you've walked over the same pathway so often, it has become clearly defined. By now, you can walk on it without even having to *think* about where you're going.

You can walk through Self-Talk Park without even being conscious of where you're walking, without thinking about the path you're carving deeper into the grass with every step you take. There's no question about where to go; in time, it has obviously become the clearest path to follow.

Now let's say that Self-Talk Park is really the programming area of your brain. The first time you get a new message programmed into your brain, it doesn't leave much of an impression, just like the first time you walked through the grass in that imaginary park.

But as you receive the same program again, and then again, the pathway begins to become clearer; the program becomes stronger. Each time the same or a similar program is repeated, you're actually sending chemical "nutrients" to specific neural pathways in your brain, and those pathways "grow" and become stronger and stronger—like building an asphalt highway, layer upon layer.

Pathways become walkways; walkways become roadways; roadways become highways; and highways become superhighways. The *smallest programs*, repeated often enough, create stronger and stronger programs, until in time, they become *super programs*.

Why is Darrel so negative? It's where he walked in Self-Talk Park. It's the result of the programs he got, repeated so often that they became the paths Darrel would automatically follow for the rest of his life.

Why is Laura constantly fighting her weight, even though there's nothing *physically* wrong with her? It was an early path she learned to follow, and one on which she continues to walk, even today.

Why is Billy having problems in school? Why can't Ken get a better job? Why does Ellen have trouble with every man she dates? Why is Peter so negative?

Why do you and I do what we do? And why don't we do what we know we *should* be doing? We all started out walking through Self-Talk Park—and all of us are walking there, still.

THERE'S HOPE FOR US YET— WE CAN *CHANGE* OUR *PROGRAMS*!

When I discovered that our futures—in fact, our entire *lives*—were up to the dictates of our programming (mostly the *wrong* programming), I could have gotten discouraged. But fortunately, my research didn't end there. It was apparent that there were people who had learned how to not only survive, but also to *excel*, in spite of their programs. I reasoned that if *they* could do it, then there's hope for the rest of us. *More* than hope. What I learned was, that although our personal computers are designed to be programmed, they are also designed to let us *change* those programs. And now we know how to do exactly that.

Chapter Three

The Programs You Have Now

Before I show you how to change the programs you got, it will help to find out what some of those programs are right now.

To do that, I'm going to ask you some of the same kinds of questions I would be asking you if I were coaching you individually. These are questions your personal coach might ask you to help you get to know *yourself* better.

As you read each question, *take the time to actually formulate a clear answer in your mind.* (It will help if you read each question twice.) Some of the most important things you'll learn as we go along will come from the *answers* you give, so the clearer your answers are, the more you'll learn about yourself. Here's the quiz about your programs:

1. On a scale of 1 to 10 (1 meaning *not* so good, 10 meaning *great*), how would you rate your programs overall? Think about that. If you had to rate the programs you have now, in general, what rating would you give them?

2. What would you say were your three strongest programming *influences* while you were growing up? These could be the people who raised you or other people who had a great influence on you. Things that programmed you could also be repeated experiences. Examples of programming influences might be: *parents, grandparents, siblings, other relatives, friends, teachers, television, church, etc.* Be specific.

3. Give two or three examples of the strongest *positive* programs you have right now. Some examples could be: *I'm a great Mom or Dad; I have a good head for numbers; I take time to relax; I'm good at dealing with problems; I'm very organized; I'm a good listener; I take good care of myself,* etc. (To find your best programs, look at what's working.)

4. Think of two or three examples of *negative* programs you have right now. Here are some examples: *I don't think I'll ever be financially independent; I have trouble with my weight; I argue too much; I can't seem to get organized; I worry too much; I'm never on time; I have low self-esteem,* etc. (To find the programs that are working against you, think of any problems you have that tend to *repeat* themselves.)

5. Do you have any negative programs right now that you would like to *change*? These may be the same as the pro-

grams you just listed above, or they could be different. If you have *any* programs that you would like to change or get rid of, what would they be?

6. What are at least two new positive programs you would *like* to have, that you feel you do *not* now have? Think about this one. Some examples could be things like: *giving yourself more free time; feeling more positive about yourself; being able to get along better with a family member; being better at math; not letting small things bother you; having better eating or exercise habits, etc.*

If you could suddenly have two or three positive new programs, what would they be?

7. Now let's find out how you would *rate* the programs you have now in specific, important areas of your life. While you're rating yourself in each of these key areas, jot down your scores on a piece of paper, so you can learn your total score, and your average, at the end of the quiz.

On a scale of 1 to 10, rate the kind of programs you have in each of the following areas of your life. (1 means *not* so good, 10 means *great*.)

Your Self-Esteem programs

These are the programs that tell you how you feel about yourself and how you *see* yourself. As an example, if you feel good about yourself overall, and always have a good positive picture of yourself, and have a lot of belief and confidence in yourself, your score would be high—a 9 or a 10.

If you're often down on yourself and not happy with who you are, you would give your self-esteem programs a low

28

rating. Score yourself as accurately as you can. Rate your self-esteem programs from 1 to 10: _____

Your programs of Personal Organization and Control

These are the programs that govern how organized or "together" you are as a person, and how much control you feel you have over what happens in your life. How would you rate your programs right now? Your rating: 1 to 10 _____

Your Health and Fitness programs

Rate your programs on how well you take care of yourself and how you feel about your size, shape, weight, health, etc. Your rating: 1 to 10 _____

Your programs about your Job or Career

These are the programs you have that govern your attitudes about your job, the specific work you do, and your long-term career path. Your rating: 1 to 10 _____

Your programs about your Money and Finances

How are the programs you have right now that determine your attitudes about money and your financial security? Are they great programs, or would you like to have better? Your rating: 1 to 10 _____

Your Personal Relationship programs

These are the programs you have that determine how well you're doing in your relationships, overall. How do you get along with people? Do you have lasting relationships? Are your relationships going the way you want them to? Your rating: 1 to 10 _____

Your programs about your Personal Growth and Development

These are the programs that tell you the importance of your personal growth, your interest in improving yourself as a person, and your overall progress. How important to you is your personal growth? Your rating: 1 to 10 _____

The programs you have about the Quality of Your Life

How do you feel about the personal *quality* of your life overall, and your success as an individual—not just in your outward life such as your work or finances, but especially *within* you? Your rating: 1 to 10 _____

8. Now, total the scores you gave yourself in each of the key program areas and divide the total by 8 to obtain your average. What is your average? _____

9. Based on the above ratings, if you could change or improve in any area, which programming area (or areas) would you work on first?

10. On a scale of 1 to 10, how would you rate your *"self-talk,"* both spoken and unspoken, on an average day? Since what we say—both to others and to ourselves internally—is a reflection of our programs, what do your own words tell you about your programs? Is your self-talk always "up," positive and healthy-sounding? Or does your self-talk suggest attitudes that could hold you back in any way?

WHAT YOUR ANSWERS TELL YOU
ABOUT *YOU*

Even a brief look at your answers to the questions on that short quiz can tell you a great deal about yourself.

As an example, your *1* to *10* overall rating of your programs in Question #1 will tell you, in general, how you feel about yourself. It will also tell you whether you feel you got a fair deal when your programs were being handed out. (Whether it was fair or not is no longer important. What you *do* about your programs from now on is what counts.)

Who *were* your strongest programming influences when you were growing up? Were the programs you received from the people around you the right kind? We can learn a lot about who we are and how we think today by recognizing who it was that gave us most of our early programs. What was *their* programming like?

When you were asked to identify two or three of your most positive programs, I hope you had so many that it was hard to know which ones to think of first. If you can easily think of a list of positive programs that you now have, consider yourself lucky. Most people don't come up with a very long list.

The easiest way to identify good programs is to look at your life and see what's working. If you didn't come up with three clear examples of positive programs that you have now, take a few extra minutes, relax, and think about your average day and what goes best for you.

It's just as important for you to know what *is* working as it is to know what's not; if you identify the programs that are making your life work, you can create more of them.

For many people, it's easier to think of programs they'd like to change or get rid of. Typically that's the list that includes habits we'd like to change, or things we do that give us problems. How did you do? If you gave it more thought, would there be any *other* programs you'd like to change?

The section of the quiz where you rated your programs in the eight key areas of your life can give you a clear picture of *why* you're doing well—or not doing so well—in any area.

We're almost always the most successful in those areas in which we have the highest scores for positive programming. The person whose programs rate a very high score in money and finances, as an example, will typically have his or her finances in good shape. The person whose money and finances programs rate a very low score will almost always be uncomfortable or often struggling financially.

In the same way, people who have the highest self-esteem scores are always the most confident, self-assured, and successful in anything they undertake, while people with low self-esteem scores find it difficult to succeed at anything. People whose health and fitness programs rate a high score have the most success eating right and maintaining good health habits. People with low scores in this area have difficulty dealing with weight and other self-created health problems.

IT'S YOUR *PROGRAMS* THAT ARE
CREATING YOUR *RESULTS*

The most important point is that *it is the programs you have that are creating the results you're getting.* If you're not happy with the results you've been getting, don't get upset with life or mad at yourself—your onboard computer has just been programmed with the wrong input to get the job done. There is a *direct* cause-and-effect relationship between the programs you have right now and how successful you're going to be in *anything* you do.

It makes sense, then, that if you want to do better in some area, *start by changing the programs.* Make sure you've got the *right* programs to get the right job done. Your programs are in charge of your *beliefs*, your *attitudes*, your *actions*, and your *results*. So to make any lasting change, start by making sure you have the programs that will help you successfully make that change.

If you know people who are having a difficult time of it, look at their programs, and you'll see why. If you see someone who moves forward and makes things look easy, you can be sure there is a set of programs that is making things work for that person.

RATING THE PEOPLE
WHO PROGRAMMED YOU

For a number of years, I've conducted an in-person seminar program in cities throughout the United States called *"The Personal Success Seminar."* During the program I hand out score sheets and ask the members of the audience to rate their own programs, just as you did here.

But I do something else that the attendees find very revealing. After each person has rated his or her own programs, I then ask them to rate their *parents'* programs (or the people who raised them). I next ask each of them to write down the names of the three or four friends with whom they spend most of their time now, and rate their *friends'* programs as well.

Almost immediately, the pattern becomes apparent. Not only do our *own* programs reflect the programs of the people who raised us, but we also often *continue* to get more of the same kind of input from the selection of people we choose to spend our time with. (If you rated each of your closest friends' programs, would *their* program scores be *lower* than yours, *higher* than yours, or about the *same* as yours?)

The message here is that unless we become consciously aware of the programs we have now, we tend to duplicate more of the same. It is only when we become *aware* of the programs we've got—and where they've been coming from—that we can take the first step toward doing something about them. We can then begin to get the *right* programs for a change, instead of continuing to get more of the *wrong* ones.

WHAT HAVE YOU PROGRAMMED
YOUR COMPUTER TO *DO* FOR *YOU?*

If your desktop or laptop computer is not programmed to do accounting or a spreadsheet, you can yell at it and pound its keys all day—it *still* won't do your accounting for you. But install a simple accounting program, and it will add, subtract, calculate, and total everything perfectly. That's what it's *programmed* to do.

When I installed a program on my computer for designing house plans, I was able to easily perform tasks which would have been difficult or impossible before I put in the new program. The result was that the right program, with my telling it what I wanted, went to work and created successful house plans. It did the job for me. It was *programmed* to.

The comparison of the success mechanism in our brain to the programming of a personal computer is not only accurate, but also clear: it tells us *exactly* what we need to do if we want to succeed.

Until your home computer is programmed with the right accounting programs, it will not succeed at math. Until my laptop was given the right architectural program, it *could not* succeed at designing a house. Until our personal *internal* computers are programmed with exactly the right success programs, they will not help us be successful—they can't!

And yet, countless people struggle to succeed without

ever once giving a thought to the programs they need to make that happen. That's why so many good people have tried one self-help idea after another, hoping they'll work, only to find that in time they didn't work at all. Why? Because even while they were trying the new self-help technique, their same old programs were busily stopping them . . . just as those programs had been trained to do!

Imagine what would happen if you changed your programs first! With exactly the right programs, there is no limit to what you could do.

That's why the story of Self-Talk is such an important breakthrough. Remember:

Change your self-talk and you will change your programs. Change your programs and you will change your life.

Chapter Four

What "Language" Do
You Speak?

In this book I've brought together the three most important personal growth tools I have ever found—and it's easy to see why one of those three tools is "Self-Talk."

Self-Talk is the term we've given to a major breakthrough in the field of personal growth. In its simplest form, *Self-Talk is a way of replacing old, negative programs that work against us—with healthy new programs that work for us.*

My own interest in Self-Talk was inspired in part by the fact that at one time I was a linguist, a Spanish-English interpreter for the U.S. in Cuba during the time of the Cuban missile crisis. At that time, if you wanted to teach a new language to someone, the best way was to send that person to a country where only that language was spoken. It's called "immersion," and it's a good way to learn a language, although not usually the most convenient way to do it. A more practical way today is to play tapes or CDs of the new language in the background. This "passive" form of learning is based on the way we learned to speak and understand our first language when we were children.

Between the time we were infants and the time we were about three or four years old, we learned a complete and complex language. And we learned it accurately—or just as accurately as the people who taught it to us spoke it—and we learned this language without attending a single day of school! It was just spoken around us, sometimes to us, but mostly it was just there, being repeated in the background of our lives.

When I began to study the research into how the programming process of the human brain actually works, I discovered that the neural pathways and networks in the brain that we used for recording the words and pictures that made up the program files of our first language, were *also* the same groups of neural pathways that we used for recording the *rest* of our cognitive programming. What we thought, what we believed, how we saw ourselves, and how we saw the world around us was all based on that same programming process. Since the recording process in the brain is the same for storing our "self-esteem" programs, as an example, as it is for something as basic as learning a language, then we should be able to record new programs of *self-esteem*—in the *same* way we would go about learning a new language.

And since learning a language is based on *repetition*, shouldn't we be able to "learn" new self-esteem programs through the same kind of repetition? Or how about our programs about *money*? Or *weight-loss*? Or our marriage, or getting organized, or our job, or anything *else*, for that matter? If we got those *old* programs through repetition, shouldn't we be able to get *re*programmed the same way— through the repetition of *new* programs?

What made this discovery so exciting was that we already knew how to learn a language! In fact, it was something we did naturally and automatically when we were children. If we could find a way to give people new programs the same way they learned a new language, then we could take the guess-work out of what to do and how to do it.

Instead of relying on unscientific practices to *try* to change programs, we could use solid, proven methods that were as old as learning itself—methods that would *work*. All we had to do was find a way to give new programs to the brain in exactly the same way it was designed to be programmed in the first place!

THE SECRET OF REPETITION

Self-improvement programs that work, and all those that *last*, always have a solid basis in scientific fact. Even though we can't physically *touch* what we think, every one of our thoughts is generated by a very physical, chemical, electrical mechanism—the human brain. If a personal growth concept doesn't adhere to the physiological functioning of our neural anatomy—how the brain works—then it's a self-help idea with no grounding in fact, and it will not last.

But from the start, Self-Talk was based on sound neurological principles—it works exactly the way our brain was designed to get programmed in the first place.

Unlike an actual computer, which needs to be told something only once for that program to be stored permanently, the human brain is designed to *learn* as it goes along—and the key to doing that is repetition. The more often something is experienced or repeated, the stronger the program is recorded or imprinted in the brain. (Like walking repeatedly through Self-Talk Park.)

WHAT "LANGUAGE" DO *YOU* SPEAK?

Let's say that John has learned a vocabulary of words and phrases (and therefore *thoughts* and *mental pictures*) that are all negative or self-defeating. Anything John thinks or says or does is going to be expressed in negative terms—because that's all he *has* in his vocabulary. So we might say that John speaks a certain "language"—in this case we'll call this language *"Failure."* Someone might say John doesn't speak our language. John only speaks *"Failure."* Those are the only words, thoughts, and pictures of himself and his world that John knows. (That's all he had stored in his "computer.")

Now let's say we know another person, Mary, who was given a vocabulary of words and phrases (and therefore thoughts and mental pictures) that are all positive and self-believing. Anything Mary thinks or says or does is going to be expressed in positive terms. That's all Mary knows. That's all she has stored in her internal vocabulary files. We'll call the language Mary speaks *"Success."* We could say Mary only speaks *"Success."*

In many ways, that's an accurate picture of what our old self-talk is. It is a *language* of thoughts, words, and pictures, a mental vocabulary that each of uses unconsciously to express our beliefs about ourselves and our beliefs about our lives. It is this language that is behind every one of our choices and our actions every day. And, of course, it's our choices and our actions that determine whether we succeed or fail. So it is our own, individual language of self-talk that, for each of us, will end up determining our successes and failures.

If you knew John and Mary personally, which of the two of them do you suppose would be doing the best at *living*, overall? John speaks the popularly-known language of "Failure," and Mary speaks the less popular, but still widely accepted, language of "Success." Mary, *because of the internal language she speaks*—because of her programs—has a much better chance of succeeding.

THE WORDS AND PICTURES YOU HAVE STORED IN YOUR MIND

It is our "mental vocabulary" which gives us the pictures that allow us to see our own lives, and to communicate both with ourselves and with others. But it goes beyond that. We don't

just think in single words—we think in practiced phrases—
thought pictures that we use again and again to identify and
catalogue the most common experiences we have.

Our lives are literally defined and governed by those
thought pictures. Our home, family, job, our habits, what we
like or don't like . . . everything we think about every one of
those subjects is immediately translated into the thought
pictures of them that we most commonly use.

*Whatever words and pictures you have stored in your
mind*—and the feelings and emotions you have that go along
with each of them—*that's it!* That's what you've got. That's
what is written on the pages of the life script that every one of
your thoughts, ideas, and beliefs comes from.

When I say the word "*home,*" what is the first picture that
comes to your mind? (What is the very first thing you think
or see?)

When I say the word "*family,*" what is the first thought
picture that comes to your mind?

Or, when I say the word "*job,*" what is the first thing you
think of? What are the feelings you have when you hear the
word?

When I say the word "*diet,*" what thought picture do you
see first, and what feelings do you have?

When I say the word "*money,*" what response first comes
to mind?

Each of your responses, and the *feelings* that went along
with them, came directly from program files that you have
stored, right now, in your brain. (If you had different program
files, you would have given different answers.)

I could give you an endless list of keywords, one by one,
and for each of them, your mind would immediately give you

a phrase or a thought picture that defined, briefly, what that keyword has just brought to your mind.

But what's even more important is that underneath, in the "unconscious" part of your storage center, hundreds *more* thought pictures—and the feelings that are tied to each of them—would fill in the blanks, creating a complete, comprehensive picture of *everything* you think and feel about that subject. All based on the vocabulary of your programs— *the words and pictures you already have stored in the filing cabinets of your brain!*

JUST LIKE IN COMPUTERS— YOUR *INPUT* CONTROLS YOUR *OUTPUT*

It must be easy to recognize, then, that if you don't have the right word phrases or thought pictures stored in your own personal filing cabinets, you won't be able to automatically come up with the right thoughts, pictures, beliefs, or actions.

John, who only has negative words and thought pictures stored in his brain, is unable to see the positive outcome of anything. So he always fails. It's not his fault. He just has *no real* picture of success or what it looks like. It's just not stored there, in his brain, right next to the file marked, "self-esteem," where it's supposed to be.

Mary, who has only positive words and thought pictures stored in her filing cabinets, will automatically see the best possible alternatives, the right choices to make, and the best possible outcomes of her actions. Her *thoughts*—her word phrases and her thought pictures—give her a completely *different* set of alternatives and possibilities than John has. John and Mary speak almost entirely *different languages*.

It's not as clearly defined in our real world, of course. We don't have 100% bad programs or 100% good programs. But the results of our programs—*whatever they are*—are just as real. If you have more negative programs working *against* you than you have the right kind of programs working *for* you, then you can predict that in most cases, the *results* will be negative.

It's no surprise, then, that the people who have the best programs are the most successful. Their internal choice-making mechanism is based entirely on their programs. So it should also come as no surprise that the people who *choose* their "language"—by *changing* their self-talk are the ones who get better programs, and the ones who become more successful.

IT'S SIMPLE ON THE SURFACE

Can it really be that simple? The process behind all this—the physiological, electrochemical process in the brain that makes this all happen—is incredibly complex, but the daily personal practice of changing our programs with the right kind of Self-Talk is practical and simple, at least on the surface.

Underneath it all, we have a very smart brain. It knows that if we're going to learn something that is necessary to our survival, we're going to have to be able to learn it in a very simple way. (It was easy to learn, "Don't touch the hot stove," for example.)

So our brain was designed to do something as important as learning our basic "life programming" in the simplest way possible—first and foremost, by *hearing* it. And we got our programs, hearing them, almost without even being aware of them, as they played again and again in the background of our lives. (*"Sharon, you're never going to be good at math." "Dennis, no one in this family will ever be rich."*)

CHANGE YOUR *INPUT*— CHANGE YOUR PROGRAMS

Imagine, then, what would happen if you used that same, simple process, that same miracle of programming *over again*. But what if this time *you* were in control? What could you do if you had the right kind of programs working *for* you—instead of the wrong kind of programs *ever* working against you?

What if you could change your *input* and change your programs? And what if this time you got it *right*?

You *can* change your input. You *can* get it right this time. And in the next chapter, you'll learn specific techniques you can use to begin taking control of your programs for yourself.

Chapter Five

Changing What You Say

What do you think of when you hear the expression *"talking to yourself"*? You may picture someone walking down the street muttering to himself, or perhaps you thought of you, absentmindedly talking to yourself.

But the Self-Talk we're talking about here is nothing like that at all. I'm going to show you that with a few Self-Talk techniques and an understanding of how Self-Talk works, you can begin making positive changes in your outlook—and in your day—almost immediately.

I'm also going to share a Self-Talk technique with you that will actually *change* old negative programs and *replace* them with the kind of programs we wish we would have gotten in the first place.

We'll start with what would appear to be the simplest

Self-Talk technique of all—*changing what you say*—the word pictures you unconsciously paint about yourself and about the daily circumstances of your life.

It makes sense that if the strongest messages we receive about ourselves from the *outside* world are stored and acted on as though they're true, then we should be *doubly* careful what kind of messages *we* give to *ourselves!*

Think how many messages you give to yourself in just one day. Think how many hours you're *with* yourself every day. It's no surprise that *you* are your #1 programmer.

The question is, when you're with yourself all of those hours each day, what are you saying to yourself about you? What are you saying to you about each of the events, moments, questions and details of living that come up each day?

What really controls your attitude as you go through your day? What do you say to yourself when you have a problem? What about when there's an argument, or someone disagrees with you? What do you say when you're supposed to be somewhere on time and you're getting late? If you happen to be watching your diet, what do you say just before you eat something you shouldn't—or just *after* you eat it?

EITHER *YOU* CONTROL YOUR SELF-TALK— OR YOUR SELF-TALK CONTROLS *YOU*

Most of what you actually say to yourself is completely unconscious—without thought. From the moment you wake up in the morning until you fall asleep at night, you can have an ongoing internal dialogue with yourself without *once* having to consciously *think* about what you're saying to yourself; you can go through the entire day with your self-talk on *autopilot*. It's like you're flying an airplane without taking the controls.

And yet, during every one of those moments throughout that day, someone or some*thing* is busy directing, managing, and controlling virtually everything about you. When you get upset at something, or eat something at lunch you're trying to avoid, or raise your voice at someone when you shouldn't, or put off doing something you know you should do, or think you're not up to the task when you know you should be . . . who do you suppose is flying the plane? Who's in charge?

Your old programs are in charge!

At those moments, you're not in charge. Your programs are. When you're not in charge of your programs, your programs are in charge of you. Either you control your self-talk, or it controls you. So, *consciously* taking control of your own self-talk, which may seem like a simple thing and not important, becomes an incredibly important step. Especially if you want to be in control of your own life, and if you want to have a chance of changing your old programs.

WHO'S *IN CHARGE* HERE?

Making the choice to be aware of every message you give yourself is an important choice. But many people, even among those who genuinely *want* to be in charge of their self-

48

talk, fail to follow through with this choice. Why? The old programs are too strong! Those programs have been in charge for *years*, thank you, and they're not about to give up their control of your life just because you read a book and decide to change.

We've all been practicing flying on autopilot for years. We've gotten good at it. We can talk to ourselves day in and day out for months without ever once stopping and saying, *"Hey! Wait a minute! What have I been saying to myself? Who's been telling me all these things about me? Who's in charge here?"*

In a previous chapter, I gave you a short list of some of the kinds of things people say out loud about themselves—examples of *negative* self-talk (. . . *I can't remember names, nothing goes right for me, I'm just not lucky, I'm so clumsy, I'm so stupid . . .*). But our *unconscious* self-talk goes far beyond those simple, self-defeating messages. How about the directions we give ourselves, called *choices*?

Our choices—made for us by our programs, instead of by our better selves—don't even have to sound negative or harmful—but they can still be just as *wrong*. When the teenager takes his first cigarette, he's not making a conscious choice to destroy his health and hurt himself for years to come. His programs are making the choice *for* him; wrong *programs*, wrong *choice*. Or how about the mother who's had a bad day and yells at her child until the child starts to cry? It is the mother's old programs—uncontrolled by her—that are doing the yelling.

Our unconscious self-talk affects everything we do, from something as seemingly small as getting cross when we're tired, to things as big as which job we apply for. Literally everything in our lives, every day, is touched by the unconscious influence of our own unconscious self-talk—and thus, by *whomever* or *whatever* gave that self-talk *to* us.

Once we know the truth of that, it shouldn't take a lot of persuasion to convince us to do something about it.

"MONITORING" YOUR SELF-TALK

There are three steps that will help you get started immediately fixing problems you might have with your unconscious self-talk. In this chapter we're going to take the first step. It's called "Monitoring."

Monitoring means to listen—*really* listen—to everything you say throughout the entire day. Once you get into the habit of doing this, you'll automatically hear more of what you're saying and what you're thinking—the kinds of messages you're giving yourself that used to be unconscious. But now, because you *practice* listening to them, you actually *hear* them—you're aware of them. It's only when you become *aware* of your old self-talk that you can begin to change it.

To get an idea of what listening to yourself actually feels like, start by having a "monitoring day." For one whole day, listen to what you say out loud, and to the things you say silently to yourself. Write notes if you have to, reminding yourself to pay attention and listen. Post the notes everywhere, so you won't be able to miss them as you go through your day. (Instead of writing, *"Remember to listen to myself,"* you may want to just draw a big check mark on the notes you post around you, so you won't have everyone else asking you what you're doing. The check mark will remind you to check yourself, and you'll privately know what it means.)

Although the step of monitoring your own self-talk is simple, it may not be easy. We're so used to *not* listening to what we say to ourselves that doing so takes some effort. To help yourself listen, here are three questions to ask yourself throughout the day:

1. *What am I saying to myself right now?*

2. *Am I saying what I really want to be saying?*

3. *What should I be saying instead?*

During the day, whether you're saying something out loud or silently, repeat those questions to yourself. Write them down and keep them where you can glance at them as a reminder.

MONITOR & MODIFY—
FIND THE *OLD* SELF-TALK
AND TURN IT AROUND

Once you begin to be aware of the internal dialogue that's actually going on within yourself throughout the day, you almost naturally begin to want to change some of it. When you realize that through the simple force of *will* you can *change* what you think—or how you *feel*—anytime you want, you suddenly sense yourself having more control, and you recognize how good it feels to exercise that control. Here are a few examples:

Try changing, *"I can't do this,"* to *"I can do this,"*—and *mean* it—and watch what happens to your attitude about the problem.

Change, *"I don't have the energy I used to have,"* to *"I make sure I've got plenty of energy—and I feel great!"* and notice how you suddenly experience a boost in how you feel.

When you catch yourself saying (out loud or to yourself) *"That makes me mad!"*—immediately change your self-talk to, *"I can deal with this. I'm cool, calm, and collected."*

Change, *"I can't figure it out,"* to *"I can think this through,"* and notice how welcome a reminder it is to remember that you're intelligent.

When you hear yourself making an excuse, like, *"I didn't have the time to get it done,"* replace the untruth with a strong, firm, *"I didn't get it done . . . that's unlike me."* When you make a statement like that, of the new kind of Self-Talk, notice how good the resolution makes you feel. (Your self-esteem will get a boost every time you do this.)

Change, *"Nothing is going right for me today!"*—to *"Today's a good day. I'm in control; I'm having a great time, and I'm going for it!"* Then see if your day doesn't start to turn around. You may not be able to change all of the external causes that are creating the problems for you that day, but you *can* change how you react to them and how they affect your attitude. And your day will start to improve as soon as your attitude does.

IMMEDIATE BENEFITS AND
LONG-TERM REWARDS

Changing your unconscious old self-talk and replacing it with a much more responsible, conscious, new Self-Talk will not, by itself, change your old programs—at least, not at all quickly. It's not designed to. Certainly, if you really get into the habit of always constructing your internal messages to yourself in the right way, they will have a positive, long-term effect on your programs overall.

But we get our programs through repetition—a *lot* of it. A lot *more* repetition than you will give yourself just by changing your self-defeating thoughts into self-*creating* thoughts as you go through the day. Some of your big programs will need stronger reprogramming than that.

However, even if this first Self-Talk technique is not designed to erase or replace all of your old troublesome programs, this technique will be extremely helpful and valuable to you from the first day you use it.

The Self-Talk technique of learning to monitor and modify your old self-talk will bring you immediate benefits and long-term rewards. Here are the results you can expect:

1. You will *stop giving yourself any more negative messages* that would keep reinforcing the negative programs you already have.

2. You will give yourself an *immediate* attitude shift and

literally change how you feel as you go through your day.

3. You will set up more success in the *future* by giving yourself a positive new direction *today*.

4. You will take the control of your unconscious thoughts and choices *away* from your old programs—and give the actual control of your life *back to you*.

When you monitor and modify, that's what you can expect. When you start actively monitoring your self-talk and changing it, your days will get better. You'll have more focus. You'll stop inviting the negatives of the past to participate in your present. And you'll put *yourself* back in control of who you are and what you want.

YOU MIGHT BE SURPRISED AT
HOW WELL IT WORKS

How much will you actually change in your life just by being conscious of your old self-talk and changing it around so it points you in the right direction? You might be surprised! Since most of our "luck" is self-created, doesn't it make sense that you have the capacity within you to turn your luck—and your day—around at any time? If that sounds like wishful thinking, what do you think would happen if you walked around all day saying, *"Woe is me, woe is me, all I have is bad luck,"* and then watched to see what happens to you that day? (That would be a bad idea. Don't do that.)

But we do the same thing when we let our unconscious self-talk go unchallenged, saying whatever self-critical or self-defeating thing it wants.

YOU'RE NOT KIDDING YOURSELF— YOU'RE CHANGING YOUR FUTURE

When you see someone who is starting to practice using the right kind of Self-Talk, consciously looking at the brighter side, being more positive, and having the courage to exercise self-confidence for no reason at all, your old way of thinking could have a tendency to deride the idea as foolish, ridiculous, or "Pollyanna," *way* too positive—unrealistic. But let's examine that reaction.

What exactly is it about us that makes us think anything good is too good to be true or too good to last? What is it within us that sees the *worst* first and the *best* last? And what makes us think that seeing the day in a whole new way is for dreamers who don't understand the hard, cruel world? What makes us *think* that way? It's our old *programs*, of course— the clouds of misgiving that darken the sunlight of possibility.

The comment frequently heard when you decide to look at things from their brighter side is, "Get *real*!" As though "real" is defined by Murphy's Law, and "bad" is the natural way for things to be. But the people who tell you to get real are ultimately missing the point. Their thinking is no more scientific or civilized than the superstitions of our earliest ancestors huddling in their caves. Circumstances of life, by their nature, are neither "bad" nor "good." They are *neutral*. It is we, the beholders, who make things bad or good.

YOU *GET* MOST
WHAT YOU *EXPECT* MOST

There is a universal law that we don't yet fully understand, but it is more real than the doubts of the naysayer. It is the law that says, *"you get most what you expect most."* The person who expects problems and calamity lives a life of chaos and failure. The person who expects the best and a promise of good things to come lives a life that *attracts* achievement and encourages fulfillment.

That doesn't mean bad things don't happen or that everything always works the way we want it to. But it does tell us that if we predict—*by our very own words*—a negative outcome, that's exactly what we can plan on getting.

INVITE IN ONLY THE GOOD

There is an old saying that tells us to *"Invite in only the good —when you invite in the bad, it will come in, and it will bring its friends."* My experience is that when you invite in the good, that's what will come in, and it will bring *its* friends.

The most successful and "complete" people I know all understand that we *ourselves* create almost all of what happens to us. There is no dark shadow of fate lurking outside the door, waiting to darken our lives with a cloak of tribulation—unless we have invited it to be there. We, by our own words (and thoughts), invite in either the good, or the bad, but *we're* the ones doing the inviting.

Why is what we "expect" an important point? Because it is our individual, programmed beliefs about our own futures that write the script we rehearse each day. It is self-evident that what we *expect* most, we *create* most. And what we expect most is best seen in the pictures we create with our own words—our self-talk.

It would follow, then, that one of the secrets to doing well, living a good, fulfilling life, and living up to your best each day would be to *expect* what you want to *get*—and make sure your own words and thoughts—your own Self-Talk—*reflect* what you *expect*.

You might want to try that tomorrow.

Chapter Six

Having a Talk with Yourself

It was many years ago that I first learned it's okay to talk to yourself. In fact, I recommend it. If you're someplace where it's private, you can even have a conversation with yourself out loud. Doing that can be revealing and helpful. And it's a great way to get into the habit of getting your Self-Talk right.

Most mornings when I'm at my home, I walk through the oak trees behind my writing studio and down to the dock. I try to do that around sunrise. The dock stretches out some distance into the water, and at the end there is a large T-shaped area with benches for fishing or sitting and talking, or for just contemplating the beauty of the place.

I like to have conversations out at the end of that dock, especially with myself. There's just me and the early morning sun, and my thoughts for the beginning of the day. I've had some good conversations there.

I've learned a lot, too. Things I would never have known if I hadn't taken the time to get to know myself better and understand what I really thought about things.

I first started having those conversations out loud with myself out in the fields where I worked in the Midwest farmlands when I was a small boy. I'm sure the other kids would have made fun of me if they had known that I spent hours talking to myself about everything under the sun. But I also know that later, even as a teenager, I never wondered who I was or where I was going with my life. I talked about that and other things that were important to me. And I listened.

You don't have to have a dock on the bay or an endless field of wheat to talk to yourself. You can do it anywhere you have some quiet or some privacy. And I'm not talking about that once-every-year-or-two talk with yourself during your vacation at the lake. This is a daily or a weekly thing, not a yearly thing.

This is a time for getting in touch, and staying in touch, with who you are—really—and what you want. It's a time for making sure you know exactly where you're going and exactly the kind of attitude you need to get there!

HAVE A TALK WITH YOURSELF

In this chapter, I'm recommending that you do something

most people, in their entire lives, do only rarely, if ever: hold a _real_, clear, honest, private, word-for-word conversation with yourself—out loud.

Why out loud? When you hold these special conversations with yourself, you should ask the questions and give your answers out loud, because in doing that you're going to hear what you really think!

When you talk out loud, it isn't as easy to muddle your thoughts and give half-thought-through responses as it is if you just think silently to yourself. You articulate your ideas more clearly when you express them out loud.

Also, when you hold a conversation with yourself out loud, you set the stage completely differently than when you're just casually thinking about something. It takes it out of the ordinary. It says, _"All right, listen up! This is the real thing. This is important, and I want your undivided attention. This is about you, and what you say next counts!"_

I've found talking to myself out loud—in the right way—so helpful, that over the years I've had some of the most rewarding conversations of my life in many different places, based on where I was at the time. Some of my conversations have been on morning walks, driving in the car, riding horseback in the mountains, driving a tractor, pacing the floor in a gazebo, on the beach, in the shower, or mowing the lawn. If you want to find a space to talk to yourself, it's not hard to do.

SET ASIDE TIME FOR YOURSELF

If you don't practice setting aside time for yourself, you will never *have* time for yourself. If you think you honestly *don't* have the time to spare for yourself, then you *really* need time for yourself. It's all a matter of what's important. And you have to make this important. You have to make *you* important.

I suggest you set aside at least half an hour for a heart-to-heart conversation with yourself. Even if you think you'll run out of things to talk to yourself about, set aside the time anyway.

A GOOD WAY TO PRACTICE
THE *RIGHT* KIND OF SELF-TALK

When you have a conversation with yourself in this way, you'll immediately notice that you're communicating with yourself in a *better way*.

Knowing what we've learned about programming and our own Self-Talk, as we've discussed here, why would we ever *consciously* say anything to ourselves that is not positive or uplifting, or does not look for the best in ourselves? (When we're *aware* of our own Self-Talk, *and are determined to improve it*, we almost *never* say things that are negative or self-defeating.)

That doesn't mean that when you have a conversation with yourself, you would ignore problems or overlook the obstacles. But when you talk to yourself in this way it's almost as though there is *another you*, speaking to yourself from a *higher* level, answering the questions and speaking back to you.

So when you have a clear, simple conversation with yourself, you automatically *practice* using the better kind of Self-Talk—and work at getting it right.

ASK YOURSELF GOOD, CLEAR QUESTIONS— AND GIVE YOURSELF GOOD, CLEAR ANSWERS

One of my typical self-conversations usually begins with me saying, *"Good morning, Shad. How are you today?"* And I usually answer back, *"I'm incredible!"* And then after commenting on what a great day it is, and how good it is to be alive, I might say, *"What would you like to talk about today?"*

What follows could be almost word for word what would be said if you were having that same conversation with your personal coach—except in this case, you're both the coach and the client.

The secret to discovering more of yourself and what you want—and what course of action to take next—is in asking yourself good questions and being willing to give yourself clear, honest answers.

Remember, you're completely safe. There's no one there

62

to criticize you, or tell you you're foolish, or point out your faults, or tell you what you cannot do. There is only you, your hopes and dreams, your trust in yourself, and your day and your future in front of you.

Practice asking yourself questions. Practice answering them—from your heart. You'll be surprised at what you hear yourself say.

THE PERSON WHO HAS THE ANSWERS

Assume for the moment that I'm coaching you personally, and for this coming week I've given you an assignment that is going to help you make rapid progress. The assignment is to spend at least thirty minutes somewhere in private, having an open, honest conversation with yourself.

The reason I'm giving you the assignment is to help you get in touch with the person who has the answers—so we can start finding out who you really are and what you really want—and find a way to help you get it.

What will make your self-conversation more comfortable and quite natural-feeling is simply to imagine that you are coaching yourself, and as the "coach," you ask the right questions. As "yourself," you give the answers. You can, to some extent, step out of yourself, like the objective outsider, much like an outside coach would be.

I want to encourage you to get in the *habit* of talking directly to yourself any private time at all. It's healthy. Along with giving you the chance to practice using the right kind of

Self-Talk, it gives you true insight into who you are and what you want. It helps you find focus. It helps you stay on track. It puts *you* in control of you—and it's *very* good for your self-esteem to feel yourself being in control.

When you have a conversation with yourself, ask yourself the same kinds of sample questions that I'm asking you here, in the book. You can ask yourself questions either in first-person (*How do I feel about myself today? . . .*), or in second-person (*How do you feel about yourself today?*). During your conversations with yourself, ask yourself questions like these:

How do you feel about yourself today?

How do you feel about doing some things to improve yourself?

What do you think you'd like to work on most?

Is there anything that you think might be holding you back from really being your best?

What do you think you'd like to do about that?

What makes you feel best about yourself?

What are some things you can think of that you'd like to do more of?

How do you think your attitude has been lately . . . on an average day?

Is there anything you can think of that you'd like to change about your attitude?

How is your Self-Talk? Is it always the way you'd like it to be?

Do you feel you're going the direction you'd like to be going?

Are you making the progress you'd like to be making?

Is there anything else you could be doing to help yourself move forward?

What's one thing you could do this coming week to make it a really good week?

What attitude do you choose to have right now?

When you take the time to talk to yourself honestly and openly, you'll start to practice using the right kind of Self-Talk, and you'll begin to hear yourself talking to you in a whole new way.

And when you answer the questions you're asking yourself, you become more aware of *who you are,* really, and what you really want—and you start to understand what to do next. This one Self-Talk exercise, even by itself, will help. In time, with practice, it becomes a habit. It opens a wonderful door to an incredible person—*you*! And it helps you keep that door open for the rest of your life.

Chapter Seven

Listening to Self-Talk

For many years, I have looked for the most practical solutions for personal growth. There have been so many seemingly good self-help ideas. But ultimately, if they aren't practical or if they demand too much time or dedication, people try them for a while, and then impatience steps in and they're put aside, like so many other good ideas in the past.

But a *few* of the ideas are different. Self-Talk is one of those. Of all the ideas I've discovered along the way, of those that worked and actually made a difference in people's lives, listening to the right kind of Self-Talk is one of the very best. In my own life, I can't imagine being without it.

I first began listening to the new kind of Self-Talk a number of years ago when I wanted to lose weight, and nothing I tried was working.

At the time, I was studying how programming works in the brain, and I knew that Olympic athletes and NASA astronauts were training with a form of Self-Talk. I thought that if it worked for them, maybe Self-Talk would help me with my goal to lose weight and keep it off.

We knew by then that our own programming determines almost everything we do (including what we eat), and we also knew that our programming comes to us most naturally through repetition. So it made sense that if we wanted to get *new* programs, we would also have to get *them* through repetition.

LEARNING WHAT WORKS

In my study of Self-Talk, and how it could help us, I explored many different ways it might be used. I was interested in learning what *works*—not just "kind of," but what *really* works.

I had experimented with printing Self-Talk on cards and repeating the Self-Talk phrases out loud. But the task of doing that was tedious and slow—and ultimately, ineffective. I also suspected that in order to create new programs that would be strong enough to override the old, negative programs, the new Self-Talk would have to be repeated more naturally, and much more often than I would have the time or the patience to do by reading phrases from cards.

I also found that the idea of posting Self-Talk cards

around my mirror could be a good reminder, but once again, just casually reading those cards could not give me the reinforcement that would be needed to make the new programs strong enough for me to reach my weight loss goal.

IF IT'S TOO DIFFICULT TO *DO*,
IT WILL NOT WORK

My study of the most successful personal growth concepts had convinced me that any self-help program which required a "ritual" that was too demanding or out of the ordinary would not work (because it wouldn't last). We're just too busy to reread repeatedly, memorize, chant, repeat affirmations over and over, or do anything else that requires a routine that gets in the way of the demands of everyday life. And none of the usual self-help methods, including reading motivational books (even several times) could deliver the kind of repetition it would take to make actual, *physical, chemical changes* in the program pathways in the brain.

I could read any number of good books about weight loss or diet or exercise, and not be one day closer to my healthy weight, because the reading of those books would not do enough to change my old programs that were keeping the weight on.

Even today, with our greater awareness of how programming actually works in the brain, some people still find it difficult to understand that we don't really change our programs by reading a book or even by attending a seminar.

But the fact is, we *cannot*. From sources such as books or seminars or other forms of teaching, we get *information*, new *knowledge*, *insights*—but not strong, mature new programs.

IT TAKES MORE THAN THAT

Reading a book, even reading it again and again, doesn't come close to creating the amount of repetition necessary to create strong new program pathways in the brain. It may *seem* like we're getting new programs from a book, especially if the ideas we're reading are interesting and helpful. But it takes more than that to give us permanent new programs—the kind we unconsciously *act* on.

Let's say, as an example, that Craig wants to quit smoking. Just as my old programs told me that losing weight was a difficult or impossible battle, or that I'd never get the job done, *his* old programs tell him he is a smoker and that no matter what he tries, he won't be able to quit. Will reading a book about not smoking help Craig quit?

The right book may motivate him to try harder, perhaps, but the book by itself will not change the programs that are *causing* Craig to continue smoking in the first place—programs that have to do with his self-esteem, his sense of personal responsibility, his programs that govern his health and physical habits, and who or what is in control of his life. *Those* are the programs Craig needs to change. And by itself, the reading of a book will not change them.

That's why you can attend an inspiring seminar or listen

to a highly motivational speaker, and although you feel jumping-to-your-feet-motivated at the moment, the exhilaration soon goes away, and you become your *normal* self once more.

The short-term motivation you feel is, in the brain, a natural chemically-induced "high" that is there momentarily, but then goes away. And your old programs—the same ones you *went* to the seminar with—step back in the minute you get home, and take over once again. They say to you, *"Okay, you've had your fun. Now it's time to get your feet back on the ground and quit dreaming! Back to reality!"*

The motivation you felt while listening to the speaker on stage didn't really change any of the old program files in your brain—it just overrode the programs for a brief time, and then *they* took over again.

It wouldn't have mattered how many seminars I attended on the subject of losing weight, because the attending of those events wouldn't have a lasting enough effect on the multitude of old programs that were strongly in place in my computer control center.

WHEN YOU TRY EVERYTHING
AND IT *STILL* DOESN'T WORK

There are countless well-intentioned individuals who, like I did with my weight, try again and again, with method after method, to fix a recurring problem in their lives, without ever getting the job done.

For instance, let's say that Maria wants to get her life more organized, so she reads popular books on getting organized and she also attends a workshop on time management and personal organization. Both the books and the workshop are filled with good advice and proven methods which, when put into practice by Maria, *should* end her problems of disorganization forever. She really cares about getting more organized, so she tries hard to make the good ideas work for her. And the ideas work—for a time.

But then Maria begins to slip back into her old, less organized habits. Within days she is no longer using most of the ideas. When you visit her a short time later, you would hardly know she had ever read a single book or attended a workshop on time management or personal organization. (Three weeks after the workshop, Maria can't find her daily planner because it's lost under a pile of papers somewhere on her desk.)

Unfortunately, Maria had not gotten rid of the *programs* that *caused* her to be disorganized in the first place. There was nothing wrong with reading the books or attending the workshop—in fact, I recommend getting all the helpful input you can. But if you have old programs working against you (like the person on a diet who still overeats), then the *real* problem—and the ultimate *solution*—is in the programs.

Imagine how Maria might have done if she had first gotten some new programs that created *internal* organization and control. It would have been a "different" Maria who read the books and attended the workshop. With different programs she would have accepted and applied the ideas easily and naturally—and they would have worked. (The old programs would no longer be fighting against her.) And this new Maria, with the right programs, would have been *successful*.

TO GET RID OF AN OLD PROGRAM— YOU *FIRST* HAVE TO *REPLACE* IT WITH SOMETHING *ELSE*

I recognized from situations like these that if we wanted to change our programs *permanently*, we would have to find a way to *replace* them. We would have to create a whole new set of programs pathways in the brain that would be so strong we would quit using the old program pathways entirely.

We had learned that to get rid of an old program pathway, you *first* have to build a *new* pathway to follow (or you'll just keep going back to the familiar *old* pathway—even if it's a bad program and the *wrong* pathway to follow).

When you create a positive *new* program path, and follow it repeatedly, it will become the *stronger* of the two. And when you follow the new program path again and again—and *stop using* the old program entirely—that old program will, in time, lose its strength, and die out. When that happens, the *old* program is no longer in *control*. The positive *new* program is. And you've *won!*

It's like creating a *detour* by building a brand new highway, so you no longer have to rely on the old highway —which was the *wrong* road to take in the first place.

You've probably seen an old road or highway that's no longer being used. It's full of cracks and weeds, and it's

72

breaking apart; it's no longer being maintained. In a similar way, you could compare that old highway to a program pathway in the brain. With any program we're continuing to use, each time the same message is repeated, we're keeping that program pathway *active*—when we repeat the program we're actually "feeding" it, nurturing it, maintaining it, making it stronger.

But when we stop *using* the old negative pathway, even if it was a strong, well-kept interstate expressway (a major program), that pathway will stop being *fed*. It's no longer being maintained or built up. Like the unused highway with its cracks and weeds, the brain's program pathway falls into disrepair, and eventually loses its strength.

How do you do that? You stop using the *old* program by first *replacing* it with a healthy *new* program—the kind of program you *should* have had in the first place. And you create that healthy new program through *repetition*.

(Scientists have learned that for an old program to even *begin* to break down, or start to lose its strength, you have to stop using the old program entirely for a period of at least three weeks—long enough for it to begin to lose its strength chemically and electrically in the brain.

It's for this reason that we've often been told it takes *twenty-one days* to change a *habit*. It takes that long for the new programs to even begin to take over, and the old programs to begin to die out—which explains why you can't instantly change your programs overnight—or just by *wanting* them to change.)

IT HAD TO BE SOMETHING
ANYONE COULD DO

I recognized that the secret to solving any of our recurring problems that were caused by our old programs was to find a way to *repeat* the *new* programs often enough that they would become permanent—but to do so in a way that would be easy to do, that anyone could do, that wouldn't take any extra time, and wouldn't require us to noticeably change our day to do it.

This would apply whether the ongoing problem had to do with weight or finances or personal organization, our job, relationships, self-esteem, or with anything else in our lives.

As I mentioned in an earlier chapter, we get our strongest programs the same way we learned our first language. I reasoned, then, that if the way we learned our first language was to *hear* it repeated over and over, in the background, we should be able to create strong new programs in any *other* part of our lives—in the *same* way.

FINALLY, SOMETHING
THAT WORKED

As it turned out, I was right. My final solution was to spend several weeks writing *very* specifically worded Self-Talk messages and have them professionally recorded. I decided

74

to test the idea of listening to recorded Self-Talk, and I decided to focus on the programs that were actually *responsible* for my weight problem in the first place.

None of the new Self-Talk that I had recorded focused on *food* or *diet*. I knew that with most weight problems, food is not the real problem—food is only a part of the symptom. It's *other* internal programs we have that are actually causing the problem. So I carefully created new Self-Talk programs that dealt with the *real* cause of the problem—programs on self-esteem, taking responsibility for myself, health and fitness, and being in control of my life.

Because I knew the best way to learn the new Self-Talk would be to receive the new messages exactly like we learned our first language, that's exactly what I did. Each morning I would play the new Self-Talk quietly in the background, while I was shaving. I didn't focus on it or try to repeat it or pay any special attention to it; I just let it play in the background. It was easy to do, and it didn't take any time out of my day.

I would also play a recorded session of the Self-Talk while I was driving in the car, or at some other time during the day. And I would play the new Self-Talk just before I went to sleep at night.

The results were remarkable! In ten and one-half weeks I lost fifty-eight pounds (while I was shaving!). What further impressed me was that my wife, who also wanted to lose weight, lost twenty-five pounds during the same time—by *overhearing* the Self-Talk I was playing for *me*, in the background.

That was now over twenty years ago. I've never had to diet again, and the weight problem never came back. The new Self-Talk *worked*—and it *stayed*. I had gotten rid of the programs that had caused the problem in the first place.

IT'S NOT MAGIC—IT'S *VERY* REAL

There was no magic in what happened to me. I just did what the brain was designed to do in the first place. Only this time I made sure I got the *right* programs instead of the wrong ones. What made it work was that I had found a way to change my programs—that was *natural*.

Since then, many other people have done the same kinds of things, with the same kind of success. But the use of Self-Talk has gone far beyond that.

Since my first Self-Talk experiment years ago, many tens of thousands of people have listened to Self-Talk recordings to help them get better programs in virtually every area of their lives. Special Self-Talk recordings for children are played in classrooms in schools. Teenagers listen to Self-Talk that gives them the *right* kind of messages about themselves —to counteract the *negative* messages they're getting from the world around them. And adults from every walk of life now listen to daily Self-Talk to create new programs for self-esteem, family, relationships, job, money, health and fitness, and personal growth.

I still listen to Self-Talk. (I no longer have to listen to Self-Talk to help me with my weight; that got fixed.) Now I listen because there will always be new areas in which I'd like to do better—new challenges to meet. We can always use

76

new programs. We can always get better.

THE *OTHER* BENEFITS OF LISTENING

There are other benefits to listening to Self-Talk—*beyond* the incredible benefit of creating new programs. One of the first things you notice is that when you listen regularly, your *attitude* gets better. You tend to be more positive. You approach problems differently and are more open to possible solutions. (Many people find they argue less and listen more.)

Experiencing an upward shift in your attitude would make sense. When you start the day hearing the *right* Self-Talk, you're setting a pattern for the rest of your day to follow.

Another benefit to listening to Self-Talk is that you feel more *focused* and *in control*, so you naturally make better choices—with less stress. And, even though the purpose of the Self-Talk is to create new programs, it also *motivates* you at the same time. So your day goes better. You stay on target. You get more done. And you reach more of your goals.

And of course, listening to the *right* kind of Self-Talk makes you aware of the kind of unconscious self-talk you've been using in the past, and you immediately begin to *edit* the negative kind of self-talk, and replace it with the right kind of Self-Talk. So you begin talking—and *thinking*—and seeing things in a healthier, more positive way.

If you'd like to get rid of programs that are working against you and get some entirely new kinds of programs, I recommend you listen to Self-Talk. It's the most practical and the most *painless* tool I've ever found for getting your programs right.*

GETTING THE BEST RESULTS

In the more than twenty years that specially recorded Self-Talk has been available, the Self-Talk itself, and even the technology, has gotten better. (The professionally recorded Self-Talk is now on CDs, which I find even more convenient and easy to use). We've learned what works best and what to do—and we've also learned what *not* to do.

Here are some personal pointers that will help you get the best results from listening to Self-Talk.

1. Play the Self-Talk quietly in the background.

Just remember how a child learns his or her first language. It's just "played" in the background of their daily lives.

You'll learn the new language of Self-Talk fastest, and most easily, if you don't try to focus on it. Also, the less extra attention you have to give it, the less actual time you'll have to take from your day. And because it's convenient, you stay with it, and it works.

---

* *You can obtain professionally recorded Self-Talk CDs online at www.selftalkstore.com.*

2. Listen at different times of the day.

The professionally recorded Self-Talk programs are specially written for *morning, daytime,* or *night-time* listening. The *morning* programs are more motivational. That is, they help you start each day on the right track, and in an upbeat frame of mind. The *daytime* sessions help you create more focus, and they help you deal with issues that come up during the day. And the *night-time* programs let you go to sleep feeling good about yourself and help you get ready for another positive day tomorrow.

Some of the times many people find best for listening include:

While you're getting ready in the morning.

While you're walking, working out, or exercising.

While you're eating. (Especially if you're working on your weight or on health and fitness.)

While you're driving or riding in the car. (Listening to Self-Talk while you're on the way to work or going to an important meeting can also give you an immediate attitude lift, and boost your self-confidence.)

While you're relaxing.

In the background while you're doing something else.

Just before you go to sleep at night.

3. Don't overdo it.

Although some people may think they need to listen to Self-Talk many times a day, you don't need to. You get the greatest benefits by listening to just two or three short sessions during your busy day. Repetition is important, but it's also important to let your mind "rest" in between.

WHEN SOMEONE *ELSE* NEEDS HELP

There are times when it is someone *else* in the household who could really benefit from getting some positive new programs. That other person could be negative or perhaps have low self-esteem—and that person may not want to accept the idea that he or she could get *better* by listening to the right Self-Talk.

Just play the new Self-Talk quietly in the background where the other person can hear it, and go about your day. Don't make an issue of it. Just let the Self-Talk play. Remember, the brain is listening—whether the person hearing the Self-Talk in the background is aware of it or not. And give it time. Many people who *used* to be negative have found themselves with positive new attitudes and lives because someone in their household cared enough to play Self-Talk in the background.

In its most simplified form, here's a summary of how our programming mechanism works:

1. When we're born, our computer-like brain comes with a brand new programming file that is completely empty and waiting to be programmed.

2. From that day on, every message we receive, everything we hear, see, think, do, say, or experience in any way is recorded and programmed *permanently* in our mental storage center.

3. The messages we receive are actually *physically* recorded, chemically and electrically, in neural pathways in the brain—and they're still there.

4. Our programs are formed by *repetition.* The more often the same or similar messages are repeated, the stronger those programs become.

5. We unconsciously *duplicate*, and *act* on, the programs we get that are the strongest. (We can hear many of those programs in the form of our *old* self-talk that we continue to repeat to this day.)

6. The "storage center" of our brain is designed to store every message we receive, whether that message is *true* or *false*. Its job is to record and store any message that gets programmed into it, whether that message is accurate or not.

7. Our brain is designed to believe and act on the *strongest* programs we have—whether those programs are right, wrong, good, bad, positive, negative, helpful, or harmful.

8. Everything we *say*, everything we *think*, and everything we *do* is based on those same programs. Everything you believe about yourself, your beliefs and attitudes about everything around you, and all of your actions—everything you do—is based on the programs you have right now.

9. By listening to repeated phrases of positive *new* messages (Self-Talk), we are able to replace old, negative programs with healthy, *new* programs—using *repetition*—in exactly the same way the brain was designed to be programmed in the first place.

10. Each time the new Self-Talk program messages are *repeated*, the *new* neural pathways that are created in the brain become *stronger*. With repetition, *those* are the programs that begin to automatically and unconsciously determine what we *think* and what we *do*, and how successful we will be.

WHEN YOU HAVE THE RIGHT SELF-TALK, THE BEST IS YET TO COME

In a perfect world, there would be Self-Talk played in every home, at least some, every day. (But then, in a perfect world, we wouldn't *need* to listen to Self-Talk. We'd already have all of the right programs.)

That one simple step—playing Self-Talk in the background of your life—may be the most worthwhile and helpful thing you can ever do for your programs. Not only for your future, but for your day-to-day life right now.

The new Self-Talk is a powerful, natural tool in our quest to change our programs, and change our lives for the better. If you're not using it already, I encourage you to make it a part of your life. When you do, I suspect you'll continue to listen to Self-Talk for many years to come.

However you choose to get the right programs—whether you monitor and modify your Self-Talk every day, practice talking to yourself and getting it right, or listening to it in the background of your life—getting the right programs is a goal well worth reaching.

I said that changing our programs—and getting the right ones—is *foundational* to every other success we have. That is true beyond words. Whatever the goal, whatever you want, the reality of achieving it will ultimately be up to the programs you have that will take you there. *Change your programs and you will change your life.* There is no better thing you can do for your future.

PART TWO

Your Goals

"Successful goal-setting follows
specific steps.

If you want your goals to work,
they have to be set and tracked
in the right way."

Chapter Eight

Setting Your Goals and Getting Them Right

Next we come to the second of our three most important ingredients to create personal growth.

This is the breakthrough called "*active* goal-setting"—a method of setting goals in a way you may never have practiced before. In fact, the method for setting and tracking goals that I'm going to share with you here is so effective —and yet, so easy to do—that I rank it as one of the most important personal success tools you will ever use.

It would be accurate to say that *none* of us can hope to do our best without setting goals and getting them right. To do that, it will help to identify how you feel about goals, the kinds of goals you set, and how important your goals are to you. So to help you get a clear picture of the role that goals play in your life right now—and what you do about them— I'm going to ask you some questions.

As I ask each question, think about what you *really* think and feel, and give yourself good clear answers, just as though you were talking to your personal coach, and giving your responses out loud. *Listen to what you say* when you answer these questions. Your answers will be important.

1. Do you set goals?

If you set goals, do you set them by thinking about them, or by talking about them, or do you also write them down? Remember, few people set specific goals, and until they learn how, even fewer people write them out—so don't feel bad if you don't do that yet. How about you? Do you set goals in any special way?

2. If you set goals, how often do you set them?

Do you ever tell yourself you're going to set goals and then not do it? Or do you ever put off setting goals until some special time of the year? Somehow we got the idea that goal-setting was something we should do only now and then. So some people, the ones who *kind of* set goals, will set a few goals on New Year's Day, or maybe on their birthday, and that's it.

There's nothing *wrong* with setting goals on New Year's Day or on your birthday; but then, it's not particularly helpful, either. Few of the people who only set goals that way actually write down dates and a plan to follow, so what they end up with isn't *really* a goal; it's an *idea*, or a *want*. It's like refining wishful thinking—when you talk about it for a while, you can see the wish more clearly, but you're not actually doing anything about *getting* it.

If you're already setting goals—and you're doing it frequently and on a regular basis—congratulations! You're on the right track.

3. What are some examples of goals you've set in the past?

What kinds of goals have you set up until now? Have they been big goals or small goals? Goals can be about anything—from what time you want to get up each day, to the job you want to get. In the past, where has your focus been? Think of some specific examples of goals you've set—big or small—whether you've reached them or not.

4. When you set goals, or think about them, what areas of your life do you usually focus on most?

People set goals in different areas of their lives—health and fitness, personal life, relationships, money, job and career, habits, personal growth—and so on. Which areas do you think about most? Which areas are most important to you right now?

One reason to make goal-setting a habit is that your life

changes, and so do your goals. So an area that's important to you at one time may be less important to you a month later or a year later—and something else will take its place. Right now, for example, maybe your career path would get the most attention. A few months ago it could have been something in a relationship, or maybe it was a goal to lose a few extra pounds or walk a mile or two every morning.

The more you make goal-setting a part of your daily life, the more naturally and regularly you'll set and adjust your goals in *all* of the key areas of your life.

5. *How do you typically track and monitor the goals you set?*

Don't feel bad if your answer is, *"I don't really track my goals."* Many people never track their goals or monitor their progress—at least not in any organized way. Other people, especially those who write down their goals, may read over their goals every week or month to check their progress. Some people keep a list of their goals in their daily organizer and do a quick review every morning.

If you don't yet track or monitor your goals, I'll give you some ways to help you learn that important habit.

6. *What do you do when you set a goal, and you don't reach it?*

When you don't reach the goal, or you miss the target date, what do you do then? Do you tell yourself you'll reach that goal some other time? Do you let it pass and forget it?

Do you immediately start over and tackle the goal again? Do you get help? Since, with most goals—if they're at all important to begin with—you care about reaching them, it's important to know what to do when you miss the target.

One of our objectives, as we set goals in an upcoming chapter, will be to make sure you have the right *steps* to follow, so you'll keep going, get past the obstacles—and reach the goal.

7. When you think about goals for yourself, do you usually think in terms of long-term "dream" goals, or shorter-term goals?

Have your goals been the "long distance" kind, goals that focus on the short term of this month or this week, or goals that fall somewhere in between? When someone asks you, "Do you have goals?" do you immediately think about something right now, in the present, or do you think about some time in the future?

Your answer will tell you a lot about what you believe a real goal actually is—and what type of goals you believe you should set.

Some people only think about the very long-term goals like paying off the mortgage, getting the kids through college, or taking a trip around the world. Other people think about getting out of debt, making a career change, or, perhaps, adding on to the house—which could fall into the category referred to as medium-range goals. Meanwhile, other goal-setters are working on things like getting up 30 minutes earlier every morning, cleaning the garage, or finishing a project they're working on—all short-term goals.

When you think about goals, which kind do you think about?

8. *Do you have any goal you've had for a long time and would still like to achieve, but it seems impossible or far off in the future?*

You may have a goal—or more than one goal—that you've carried around with you for years but haven't really done anything about yet. If so, what is it? Is it a goal that you'd still like to do something about?

9. *When was the last time you spent an hour or more thinking or talking specifically about you—and about your goals?*

Think about this one. This doesn't mean talking about your goals casually for a few minutes in a random conversation. This question asks you when the last time was that you *focused* entirely on you and on *your* goals.

I've had people tell me they couldn't remember when they had *ever* just focused on themselves and on their goals. And that's not unusual. One of the reasons coaches help their clients focus on themselves and on what they want—and then help them set the right goals to achieve it—is because most of us are conditioned *not* to spend time on ourselves.

And yet, how can we possibly become the quality, focused, confident, actualized individuals we were born to be, if we don't take the time to figure out who we really are and what we really want? That's not self-indulgent or self-centered. That's *essential*.

So your answer to this question is very important. When *was* the last time you spent seriously talking about *your* goals long enough to get a clear picture in your mind about what you really want and how you can go about getting it?

10. Would you like to set goals—and reach them?

If you'd like to set goals and see the results, you can—and you're going to get some help. Reaching goals time after time isn't luck. People who set goals and reach them aren't special; there's not a "winning" goal-achievement gene that some people are born with, and other people are not. Setting and reaching goals is a simple and practical process—and that includes developing the *attitude* that will help you succeed.

I would encourage you to *go for it*. Why *not* do it? The difference between people who set goals and get good at reaching them, and people who don't master their goals and just hope for the best, is nothing more than a few simple steps that anyone can follow.

Most of us weren't taught the basic skills, so we didn't develop the habit. But's that's something you can change. All you have to do is make the choice to set goals, decide you can do it, take the first step, and *enjoy* it!

Chapter Nine

What the Right Goals
Can Do for *You*

I wouldn't be writing these words to you if I hadn't learned the right way to set goals. It was because of setting goals that I was able to write my first book—and it was other goals that created each of the eleven books that followed. What I thought at the time to be impossible was not impossible at all; the dreams I sought proved to be exactly as real and as possible as the goals I set to turn those dreams into reality.

For many years I have taught and written about qualities of the mind that are scientific and provable. Yet, I could not begin to adequately list the benefits that setting goals seems to almost miraculously bring to people's lives.

WHEN YOU SET THE GOAL—
YOU MAKE IT REAL

When you set a goal, you set positive forces in motion, forces that are so strong they can often overcome all odds. When you set the goal, you make it real.

When we see the *results* our goals create, it's easy to think there is some magical force within them, giving them strength. So much so that some goals almost seem to have a life of their own. It's as though when you write them down, and visualize them coming true, you breathe life into them, and they become real.

There are people who may not believe in this hidden power of goals. (Just as there are those who, in the face of overwhelming evidence, will not believe in the power of prayer.) But it's there, just the same. Anyone who sets goals faithfully, and watches what happens, will attest to this power. By the setting of the goal, it's as if you are drawing together all of your creative energies, all of your best choices, all of your hidden resources, and combining these with a universal source of energy that works to achieve the most positive possible outcome.

On a very practical (and scientific) level, all of this makes perfect sense. When you set a goal and put energy into it, you are in fact bringing together an incredible team of resources —and not all of them at the conscious level. It's like saying to your own internal goal-seeking squadron, *"O.K., team, this is it. This is the goal. All of you know what to do. Now, go*

93

to work on it!"

WHAT MAKES *"ACTIVE"* GOAL-SETTING WORK SO WELL?

Why does the kind of goal-setting we're talking about here—*active* goal-setting—work so well? It's true that by writing out the goal, we're imprinting a new set of "commands" into our subconscious mind—but it's much *more* than that. When we take a closer look, we find that *this* kind of goal-setting has the power to change our lives and our futures because it changes so much about *us!* This is what the seemingly simple process of active goal-setting actually does:

1. Setting goals lets you know what you really want.

Sometimes you may not even *know* what you want. Going through the simple steps of setting goals will tell you what you want—and what you *don't* want. If you're setting a goal and you find you're having to force yourself to even write it down, it's time to *re*-examine the goal. Like the reluctant bride who cannot force herself to make the wedding arrangements, we go hesitantly and unwillingly down the path that is not of our choosing.

The goals which are the easiest to write down, and the ones we look forward to working on, are the goals we invariably want the most. And the goals we want most, and put our energies into, are the goals we reach.

2.   Setting a goal—writing it out—gives you a vastly superior road to follow.

One of the most important benefits of active goal-setting is that when you define what you want and write out a plan, you almost always end up with a wiser course to follow —when you set a goal, in the right way, you have a plan. You know where you're going, and you've got a better way to get there.

It is a great loss when people wander through life hoping for the best, but then turn a deaf ear to their wiser selves within—and wonder why they're not really living the life they *could* have lived.

There is a voice inside us that may have been waiting in silence for years. But when we go through the awakening steps of setting goals, that voice, so wise and caring, once again talks to us, and it says, *"Let's look at where you're going my friend—let's talk about what you're doing with your life. What are you doing right now? What would you like to do next?"*

When we start setting goals, we begin to call on our internal sense of direction, the compass that was designed to show us the path, to lead us to our greater selves. It is a voice that used to talk to us long ago, when we still believed in our dreams. But we've been too busy, and the world has been too noisy for us to hear what the voice was trying to say. Now we begin ro reawaken that part of us that was born to *believe.*

It is when we follow our new goal plan that we begin to

feel a sense of purpose—a sense of "rightness." We get the feeling that our life is on track, and that we're finally headed in the right direction.

Is that our imagination running away with us, just wanting to believe? No, it's very real. It's the way the brain was designed to take care of us in the first place. And it's what happens—naturally—when we set goals.

3. Goals help you make the right conscious choices. And a thousand <u>other</u> choices you're not even aware of.

You can only make the best choices if you have a clear picture of what you want. When you define your *goals*, you define what you want you see the picture, and it's *clear*. You know what to do next. When you know exactly what you want and what to do each day, you naturally begin to make better choices—the *right* choices! Goals give you clarity. Clarity helps you make good choices.

But setting goals takes your choices to another, deeper level—to the thousands of choices you make that are entirely *un*conscious.

On an average day, when you haven't set specific goals, your computer control center is filled with undirected activity, busily making small, but important, choices for you without you even being aware of it. It's simply following the programs that were programmed into it by your past, by your unconscious self-talk, and by the random input from the world around you.

So, while your computer may be making a thousand little choices *for* you in a day, it's just running you around like a

96

battery-powered toy car with no one at the controls—being busy, not really guiding you anywhere in particular, making you tired, and not necessarily going in a direction you'd like to go. In fact, nobody *told* it where to go! (Other than, get up, go to work, go home, watch TV, go to bed . . . .)

But when you set clearly defined goals, you're putting your unconscious choices on notice. You're saying, *"This is what I want. This is exactly where we're going. This is what I want you to do for me."*

What happens next is a "call to action" of the mind. Like a missile that has been programmed to seek out its target, this computer-like goal-seeking facility of the human brain silently and untiringly works to reach the goal that *you* set. It watches for advantages, puts you into action, and sets up your choices for "find and achieve."

As though you're following the precise steps of a pre-programmed, master plan, you end up taking action, moving past obstacles, fine-tuning your direction, step after step, choice after choice, until the goal is met. Now the choices you make—even your unconscious choices—have *purpose.* They are *guided, directed,* by the positive objective of the goal that you set.

It's no wonder that when we set goals it seems like miraculous things start to happen for us! That's what our powerful, biochemical, mental computer control center does for us—automatically—*when we tell it what we want it to do.* That's what it does when we set goals.

4. Setting goals puts <u>you</u> back in charge of your own life!

As we just saw, you can be certain that if you're not setting goals—setting your direction for *yourself*—someone or something *else* is setting your direction for you. It is a fact of human psychology that people whose lives are not *self-*directed, live lives that are directed by the world around them. Your job, your mate, your friends, your family, your health, your finances—anything and everything around you—can contribute to the pushes and pulls that determine what you do with every single day.

Without you in control of your goals, the rest of the world is in charge. But *with* goals, *you* put *yourself* back in charge. So you know who you are. You know where you're going and what you have to do to get there. Instead of living your life based on the whims of others, you live your life based on your own best choices—your right to set your direction for yourself.

That doesn't mean you simply go your own direction and exclude all others. It means you have a direction to go—and it *isn't* based on which way the wind happens to be blowing at the time. It's based on *you* and what *you* choose. It's based on your goals.

5. *Goals show you more of who you really are—and the incredible things you can do. They bring out the best in you.*

When you take the time to set goals, you're also taking the time to ask yourself what you're capable of—what your qualities are. What are your skills? What natural talents do you have? What *could* you do if you wanted to?

When you set goals, you start to see the limits you've been putting on yourself in the past. You begin to imagine what you could do if you got rid of those limitations. Your goals will help you see farther and have more *vision* and more *belief* in yourself. Your goals are more than targets to aim for; your goals will tell you what you *can* do.

Many of us go through years of our lives without ever knowing what we're really capable of. Since we don't *have* to perform beyond average, it's easy to justify being no better than the person we've been so far, and letting it go at that. But when you set goals, you start to dream more, the positive, healthy kind of dreams that show you what you *could* do—and you see more of the potential you have inside of you.

That same wonderful picture that is filled with so many possibilities has a positive price attached to its achievement; it requires more of the *real* you to come forward to earn the reward—and that may require more talents or skills or abilities than you've had to use before. To reach the goal, you call upon the better parts of your own self. And when *all* of you is brought to life, you're a better person for it. You're doing it! You're going for it. You're *alive!* And it shows in everything you do! When you set goals, you recognize more of your potential and bring out the *best* in *you*. Your goals are a picture—in advance—of the real you being brought to life.

6. Goals bring the positive into your life!

No one sets a goal to *fail*. Good goals are *always* designed to help us get *better!* So it's only natural that *all* of our goals deal with creating more of the positives in our future. What a healthy, uplifting addition to our lives!

If you want to experience an immediate *lift* in your attitude, set a goal! If you want to feel better about the future, and honestly feel that you can expect the *best*—set a goal. (*People who set goals are more positive. People who are positive set more goals.*)

There is enough of the negative in the world around us—and often in our old programs—to stop almost anyone from believing in the beauty and the quality of life. But it's there. You just have to seek it out. You have to bring it to you. When you set goals, that's what you do. You invite in the good—and the good brings its friends.

THE REAL MAGIC

The real magic in *active* goal-setting, is that this one, positive pursuit brings together a team of powerful, internal re-sources—and puts them all to work for you. Everything from your dreams and wants to your unconscious choices and your hidden talents gets into the act. When you set goals, you harness the energy of your spirit and enlist the support of your own self-belief. You give yourself a path to follow and the directions for each step you take.

If you want to make your life work better, make the choice to set goals—and set them in the right way. With the unique method of *active* goal-setting we're using here, the positive results you get may seem like a miracle—but they won't be an accident.

Chapter Ten

Making it Easy

When I first studied goal-setting, and followed its history through the past several decades, I was surprised to learn that much of what we were being taught about setting goals was unfounded.

Early goal-setting ideas from the 1950s and 1960s were being handed down from author to author, who, in turn, and without really studying the ideas themselves, passed the same ideas down to other authors who repeated them in their latest books. The result was a rather unscientific grab bag of goal-setting rules, many of which are still circulating today as truth—but have no real basis in fact.

The problem with this is that people who would have otherwise set and reached their goals without too much difficulty, ended up having trouble because they were doing it wrong. The result was that they didn't reach the goals they had set, and they eventually stopped paying attention to serious goal-setting altogether. Among those who tried goal-setting and wanted to make it work, many of them thought *they* had failed, and gave up. It wasn't their fault. They were simply using methods that had never really been studied or proven to work.

MAKING GOAL-SETTING
EASY TO DO

As I continued to study goal-setting methods and monitor the results people were getting, I also found there were some techniques that *worked*—virtually every time they were practiced. There were actual goal-setting "rules" that proved to be accurate—and together they created a better way to set goals.

As you have seen, we now call this *"active goal-setting"*—the kind of goal-setting that helps you set and track your goals *actively*, with an action plan and a clear schedule (instead of setting goals *passively*—and then just hoping for the best).

In actual practice, the rules I discovered not only worked, but also made setting goals so easy and straightforward that anyone could do it. With these updated rules, people could count on getting the right kind of results every time they followed the steps that were suggested to them.

Some of the rules I'm going to outline for you here may

sound different from what you may have been told in the past. But you can take heart in knowing that what I share with you here has been tested in practice by many thousands of goal-setters, from every walk of life.

These rules of active goal-setting—and the specific goal-setting steps that follow—represent the best of the methods for setting and reaching goals that I have found. They have proven themselves to work—and you can count on them.

I think you'll like how easy this process can be, once you begin. I'm going to bring you completely up to date, take all of the mystery out of setting goals, and show you what to do. The more you understand these few, basic rules of setting goals, the better you'll do. Here's what we now know:

1. Goal-setting is a skill. It has to be learned.

None of us was born knowing how to set goals. Goal-setting is a *skill*—something we have to learn. Just like riding a bike, learning to swim, and learning how to drive a car are skills, we have to *learn* how to do them before we can get good at them. How well did you do the first time you tried to ride a bicycle without anyone holding you up? How well did you swim the first time you tried? How was your driving the first time you got behind the wheel?

We're fortunate that goal-setting *is* a skill, and not a talent. That means that *anyone* can learn how to do it. And as it turns out, goal-setting is both one of the *easiest* skills to learn, and one of the most *important*.

2. Small goals are more important than big goals.

Somehow, when people first started setting goals in earnest, and motivators first began telling us how important goals were, it became popular to focus on the *big* goals—the major lifetime accomplishments—and the smaller goals were overlooked. The idea of identifying and setting goals made people think of lofty achievements like becoming a millionaire or traveling the world.

But what goal-setters just a few decades ago often overlooked is that even the greatest castle is built one stone at a time. And as we have discovered, it is those single stones—each one a small goal in itself—that actually create the successes we achieve.

Even when we were taught that we should all set three categories of goals—long-term, mid-term, and short-term goals—the emphasis was placed on the importance of the long-term goals, and the highly important short-term goals were downplayed or overlooked.

Now we understand that while a long-term goal may serve as a light to follow, shining in the distance, it is the short-term goals—daily, weekly, and monthly goals—that get us there. There's nothing wrong with setting important life goals; they are the stars on the horizon that keep us headed in the right direction. But it's the small steps we take in between, day after day and week after week, that move us onward to the greater goal.

The most successful goal-setters write clear goals and action steps that tell them exactly what they're going to do this *month*, this *week*, and *tomorrow*. They're aware of the distant target—they don't lose sight of it—but when it comes to what to do and how to do it, they focus on *now*.

To help you get good at setting goals, and reaching every goal you set, practice focusing on near-term goals: *Making the phone call. Writing a list of ideas for Monday's meeting. Reading a book. Asking for input from an expert. Setting the appointment. Organizing your work space. Getting up a half-hour earlier . . . .*

Can those kinds of small, simple things change your world? Yes, they can. That's exactly how it's done.

3. All goals—that are real goals—have to be written down.

If a goal is not written down, it is not a goal. It may be a great idea, or a wish, or a want, or a whim, but it's not a *goal*. At least, not in "*active* goal-setting," the way that we now understand goals and how to reach them.

It doesn't make any difference how important your idea is. If you say you have a goal, but then do not write it down— along with a simple action plan to reach it—your chances of actually reaching that goal are extremely *low*. (Studies have shown that when a goal is *not* written down, your chances of reaching that goal are somewhere between 3% and 7%. Not very good. But the moment you write the goal down, along with a simple plan to reach it, your chances of reaching the goal increase to as much as *70 or 80%.*)

Does the simple step of writing down your goal, along with a brief action plan, actually make that much difference? That *is* the difference.

4. Written goals should begin with the word "To..."

There is an easy way to write any goal and always get it written right. Just do this: always begin your stated goal with the word *"To..."*

I'll give you an example. Let's say you want to lose 15 pounds. Write the goal like this: (My goal is...) *"To lose 15 pounds in a safe and healthy way."* Or you may want to write it, *"To weigh 135 slim, trim, attractive pounds."* In either case, you begin the goal statement with the word *"To,"* and then follow that with a verb . . . and your goal statement almost writes itself for you.

Here's another example. We'll say that you're going to set a goal to stop spending time with negative people. You would write, *"To stop spending time with negative people or listening to the negative opinions of others."* Or say you want to set a goal to take a course in Spanish in night school. You would write the goal as we've just described . . . *"To take a course in Spanish in night school."*

Well-meaning, but misinformed, goal teachers in the past often told us to write our goals in the *present* tense, like affirmations . . . *"I am financially free and at peace with my life and the world around me."* That may be a fine affirmation, but it's not a well-written goal. Goals are specific targets, and they have to be defined in clear, specific terms. Try this instead: *"To be debt free and have $150,000 in the bank."* Or, as an example, if your goal is to spend more time with your teenage son or daughter, be specific: *"To spend a minimum of three hours each week with Kelly."*

Make sure the goal is complete, but keep it clear and keep it short. With a little practice, you'll find yourself writing and stating your goals clearly and simply. Just ask yourself the question, "What is the goal?" When you answer, just start with the word *"To . . ."*

5. *All goals have to be dated with a specific date.*

Some people hesitate to date a goal with a specific date —the date by which they'll reach the goal. They feel that ties them down, or they might fail if they miss the date. But if a goal isn't given a specific date, it really isn't a serious goal. *"Soon," "whenever I can," "next month," "this summer," "or "sometime next year,"* is not going to get the job done.

When we practice writing *your* goals, I'll be asking you to date each one of them with *specific* target dates. When you do that, you're saying to yourself, *"This is the target. I know my goal; I have the plan to reach it, and I know exactly when I choose to reach my goal."* Even if you're not 100% sure you can reach your goal by the date you set (and no one can be 100% sure), set the date that you *intend* to reach the goal. And if you're concerned about reaching the goal on target—or missing the target and failing—you'll appreciate the next rule.

6. *Goals should be written to be changed, when necessary.*

Even as recently as a few years ago, goal-setters were still being taught to ". . . write your goals in *stone* and your action steps in *sand*." Meaning, that once you commit to a goal, that's *it*. By that reasoning, once you've set the goal, there's no stopping, no turning back, and no changing direction. And along with writing the goal itself in stone, you would write each of the action steps in sand, because you have to stay flexible in what you do next. It sounded good, but because of human nature, it didn't work.

The early rules of setting goals failed to take into account that life happens, and no matter what we try to do about it, there will always be unexpected circumstances we have to deal with.

The reason we were once told that goals should be carved in stone was, of course, to give us a sense of commitment, an unwavering determination to reach the goal. And it seemed as though the best way to do that was to make the goal inviolate and unchangeable. What happened in actual practice, how-ever, was that instead of people creating an unswerving commitment to the goal, when enough obstacles got in the way, they gave up in defeat instead of changing or *updating* the goal.

WHEN WE DON'T *UPDATE* THE GOAL, WE GIVE UP TRYING TO *REACH* IT

What do you suppose happens when the average individual sets a goal, stumbles, tries again and has another setback, and tries again? By a quirk of human nature, after most people have tried three times to reach a goal, and don't make it—*they give up!* They believe they have failed, and they quit. What actually happened was that life got in the way. But instead of updating the goal, changing it as necessary, or willingly setting yet another target date, they stopped. And all because they believed they had *failed*. They hadn't failed at all . . . at least, not until they quit.

Ultimately, with most goals, it isn't the completion date that counts the most—it's whether or not you reached the goal! Think back for a moment on some of the things you've accomplished that took patience and work. Let's say that for someone it might have been finishing school and getting a degree. Now, even a few years later, was the *date* of the degree important? Not usually. It's the accomplishment itself that's important. Or how about the man or woman who worked hard, got in shape, and finally lost the 35 pounds? Was the date important? Or was it the achievement itself, and the better health that followed? It wasn't the *date*—it was the accomplishment that counted.

Being willing—and ready—to change the goal or change the end date when life demands it doesn't mean you're not taking the goal seriously, or that you're not being responsible. It means that you set a target, you do your absolute best to meet the date, and if you cannot meet it—you do not quit.

Rewriting the old rule, we would now say that the *goal*, too, should be written in sand. Change it. Update it. Every week if you have to. But stay with it until you reach it.

(An exception to the rule that goals should be written to be changed is in the setting of business goals. Because many factors in a business organization may depend on reaching goals on schedule, business goals are usually set with specific dates that are firm.)

7. A "goal plan" should always include obstacles and action steps.

A good goal plan has three parts:

a) The written *goal*

b) The *obstacles*

c) The *action steps*

Pay special attention to the obstacles. When you write a short list of the obstacles you have to overcome to reach the goal, writing the action plan is easy. Here's how it works.

Let's say Anthony wants to take a trip to Thailand. He's studied a lot about Thailand, and even though it will take some effort, he really wants to go there and see the country on foot or by bicycle and get to know the people firsthand. So Anthony writes out his goal like this:

GOAL:
To spend two weeks visiting Thailand.

Next, after he has written down the date, because Anthony wants to make sure he reaches this goal, he lists each of the main obstacles that could stand in his way. He finds three of them, and he writes them down like this:

OBSTACLES:
1. I need to find or save the remaining $1200 of the $3500 the trip will cost.

2. I'm not sure I'm in the physical shape it might take to travel through the country without a car.
3. I have to find a way to get the time off from work.

The three obstacles that Anthony has identified are the key to his entire goal plan. Now that he knows what he has to deal with, he can easily define what he has to do next. To do this, after listing the obstacles, Anthony writes a simple list of "Action Steps"—the steps that will create the solutions to the obstacles.

As an example, to deal with the obstacle of having to find the money, Anthony writes:

ACTION STEPS:
1. Make a list of things I don't need and sell them on the Internet. (date)
2. Call my insurance agent and find out the cash value of my life insurance plan. (date)
3. Put in overtime at work between now and the time I leave.

Anthony would then continue on in this way, dealing with the obstacles with specific action steps, and tackling each of them. All of them practical. All of them simple steps.

What most people would only have dreamed of doing, and then discarded as nothing more than that—a *dream*—Anthony turned into reality. Now, when he shows his friends the photographs from his trip to Thailand, they think he's lucky. He's not. He just knew how to set a goal, and he followed the right steps to reach it.

111

8. The "action steps" are more important than the goal itself.

This one is key. *It isn't the goal—it's the action steps that count.* People were taught for years that the secret to reaching a goal was to develop *passion* for the goal. With enough passion, so the theory went, you would create so much desire to reach the goal that nothing could stop you. A burning desire, we are told, will do that.

I agree that the emotional energy created by passion and desire can move mountains and topple nations. But if you want to be able to set goals and reach them with any certainty, be prepared to trade "passion" for some simple, well thought-out action steps. It isn't the burning desire that gets us to the goal; it's the action steps.

Why hasn't relying on burning desire gotten people to their goals? Because many of our goals—even important ones—aren't always things we can get excited about. Buying a dream home can create a great deal of desire, but smaller goals often do not. (For most people, cleaning the basement or paying off a credit card does not typically create great passion.)

It never hurts to have passion and desire for those things in life you want most, because enthusiasm creates energy, and that keeps us moving and believing. But your goals will be best served by enthusiastically following the action steps that will take you there.

9. All goals are steps to something else.

The goal is not king; all goals are nothing more than steps to something else. This rule helps us demystify goals, and put them in their proper place. When you the remove the goal from its throne, and see it for what it really is, it becomes more attainable, less distant or out of reach.

I was making this point during a seminar I was conducting on goal-setting, when one of the people attending rose to his feet to ask a question. "What about graduating from college?" he asked. "Isn't that a goal in itself?" I agreed that it was a great goal, but that it was really nothing more than a step toward something else. In the case of graduating from college, I suspect the speaker at the college commencement address might have said that it was a step toward *everything*.

The point is that it is unlikely that you can find any earthly goal that is a final goal. All of them are steps to something else. And it is from this understanding that we can see why people who get good at setting goals seem to be so successful overall. They're constantly growing in area after area of their lives. They're moving forward, goal after goal, step after step. To them, it's not just one or two big goals that count. Each goal they set is a step to something else.

10. All goals should be tracked on a schedule.

Some people write down their goals, and that's the end of it. They've probably helped themselves some, but if they really want to reach the goal, they're going to have to do one more thing—they'll have to find out how well they're doing.

Tracking your goals can be as easy as reading them over—something I recommend you do, briefly, once each week. It only takes a few minutes to do this, but it brings the goals back into focus; it puts them up front in your mind and reminds you of the action steps you're going to take each week, or that day, to make sure you stay on track.

This is when you make sure you're taking each of the action steps, and when you find out if they're the right steps. If they're not, this is the time to change them. When you track your goals on a schedule, you'll know what's working and what to do next.

The important thing is to review your goals on a regular schedule—at the same time each week, or even daily, such as, a few minutes each morning as you get ready (and get your mind ready) for the incredible day ahead.

Those are the rules of active goal-setting. None of them is difficult, and they all make sense. When you set a goal, no matter what it is, if you follow those simple rules, you will greatly improve your chances of success.

Setting goals is the beginning of a life that works. Using those rules, and the few steps that follow, is a good way to get started.

Chapter Eleven

The Eight Important Steps

To set goals like an expert, right from the start, there are only a few steps to follow. These steps for active goal-setting will give you the simple formula that is used by the most successful goal-setters. For some time it has been their secret; now it's yours.

Step #1 — Identify the goal.

With a little practice, you'll be able to identify, in a very short time, each of the goals you want to set. People used to struggle with this one—trying to figure out what they really wanted, and whether or not it qualified as a real goal. We've learned how to make identifying your goals much easier by looking at the type of goal and how important it is to you.

Your goals will always fall into one of two categories: goals of *necessity*, or goals of *enrichment*.

GOALS OF "NECESSITY"

Goals of necessity are brought about by something happening in your life—often a need or a want that you feel compelled to do something about. That might be a goal to put more money in your savings account every month, keep your desk more orderly, go out to dinner with your spouse every week because you don't feel you're spending enough time communicating, or working out for twenty minutes four times a week.

Every goal of necessity is brought up by things that are happening in your life—things that need improving or taking care of. They're usually connected to taking care of external responsibilities that need attention.

GOALS OF "ENRICHMENT"

The second type of goal—*goals of enrichment*—is just as important as goals of necessity. Goals of enrichment grow from your own internal desire to improve your life or expand your horizons. These might be goals such as going back to school, taking up painting, traveling, doing volunteer work, joining the choir at church, making the time to read quietly, or taking time for yourself each week.

But how do you identify which goals you should actually set? What do you commit to a written goal and a plan, and what do you leave on the shelf—along with wishes and good intentions?

In any situation, ask yourself the question, *"What do I really want?"* Sometimes you have to ask yourself that same question several times, thinking it through, before you finally start to figure what it is you *really* want.

Here's a list of self-questions that will help. Anytime you're working on your goals and trying to define exactly what goal you really want to write down and work on, reread each of the questions on this list and answer them for yourself.

1. *What do I really want?*

2. *Is this something I really want to accomplish—or do I just think I want it?*

3. *Is this a goal of necessity—something I need to do, or is this a goal of enrichment—something I want to do for other reasons?*

4. *When I reach this goal, will it still be as important to me as it seems to be now?*

5. *When I reach this goal, how will it help me (or someone else)? What will the benefits be?*

6. *Is this exactly what I really want, or am I settling for something less than what I would really like?*

7. *Is this a goal I can reach? Why?*

8. *Am I willing to pay the price to reach this goal?*

9. *Is it worth it?*

10. *Is this something I'd like to work on now?*

11. *Am I willing to write this goal down and follow the steps for reaching it?*

12. *Is it my choice to reach this goal?*

When you read those questions, use the technique of reading each question twice. Answer first whatever comes to your mind. Then rethink it, and give yourself the best, clearest answer you can—the truth as you know it.

To illustrate the value of doing this, try it right now. Think of any goal you might want to reach, and get a picture of it in your mind. Then go back and ask yourself a few of the questions from that list again, and notice what happens the second time you answer each question.

Step #2 — Write it down.

As we've learned, your goal statement should always start

with the word *"To . . . ."* Decide what you want, put it in words, keep it simple, and write it down. The moment you do that, you begin to give life to your goal.

Step #3 — Write down the date to reach the goal.

Write down a specific date for the completion of the goal. If you don't know the exact date you'll reach the goal, get as close as you can. (Remember, you can change it.)

HOW DO YOU DATE A GOAL THAT HAS NO *SPECIFIC* TIME OF COMPLETION?

With most goals you can set a specific target date: *"To visit Uncle Ron and Aunt Ramona." "To have $12,000 in my savings account." "To paint the garage." "To bench press 240 lbs." "To mail out the invitations." "To get my broker's license."* A specific date—*day*, *month*, and *year*, can be applied to any of those goals.

However, there are goals that will not have precise moments of completion. They're called "progressive" goals.

As an example, the goal *"To spend more time with my friends"* would not call for a specific day or calendar date to reach the goal. It's an ongoing, progressive goal that isn't reached just once, at some precise date.

The same would be true for goals such as *"To become a better listener," "To learn to play the piano," "To stop saying negative things about myself,"* *"To get more organized,"* or *"To stop and smell the roses."*

How, then, with good goals like these, do you apply a specific date to the goal, since setting a date is essential?

The answer is to add a simple statement that reads, *"I will see noticeable progress by . . ."* and then write in the date. Let's say as an example, that you want to become a better listener, so you write that as your goal: *"To become a better listener."* Then, to date the goal, write in the date by which you intend to be able to see a clear improvement in how well you listen. (In this case, to find out if you reached your goal to become a better listener, ask anyone who knows you.)

The same simple step will allow you to date any goal you set that has no specific day or moment of completion.

Step #4 — List the *obstacles* to reaching the goal.

As I've pointed out, this step is the heart of active goal-setting. It is the short list of obstacles that leads to the action steps needed to overcome them.

I've found it works best to write your obstacles as naturally as you think of them. The person who writes down the goal, *"To learn Spanish well enough to travel on my own in Spain,"* for example, might then write down the following obstacles:

1. I didn't do too well when I studied Spanish in high school.

2. I'm not sure I have the time right now to devote to studying.

3. I would need to find a good Spanish course on CDs.

All of those obstacles are written naturally, but clearly. When you're writing the obstacles to any goal you set, just be yourself and write down anything that comes to mind. Let's say your goal is, *"To get more organized."* You might list the obstacles as:

1. I'm not sure how to get started.
2. I get organized for a while, but then I always let things slide back to the way they were.
3. I feel like I'm always too busy to take the time to get organized.

In this example I listed three obstacles. There is no rule as to the number of obstacles to list, but I've found that a short list of obstacles works better than a long list, and feels less challenging. Try to limit the list to those obstacles that are important enough to be dealt with—those that require an action step to fix them.

If you reread the previous example, you can imagine for yourself the kinds of action steps a person who wants to get organized might take. Once the obstacle is written down, and you read it over and think about it, you'll notice that the problem almost immediately becomes less intimidating, and the solution is often obvious. The key is to remember that it's the list of obstacles which will always tell you what action steps you need to take to reach the goal.

Step #5 — After each obstacle, write and date the *action*

steps you're going to take.

The action steps you write down will always tell you what to do next. As we just saw, once you've written down the obstacles, it's a simple matter to identify what action steps to take.

If you don't know what action step to take, write down: *Find out what action step to take.* That, in itself, is an action step. Then give yourself a few days or the time it takes to research the problem and find the solution. Call a friend, get on the Internet, do some research, look up the right book, find an expert . . . there is *no* obstacle you can find that *someone* doesn't have an answer for.

(Each action step is actually a small goal in itself. If you come up with an action step that is so big it has obstacles of its own, then take it out of the "action step" category, and rewrite it as a separate, full-fledged goal.)

THE ACTION STEPS WILL TELL YOU
IF YOUR GOAL IS REALISTIC OR *NOT*

When I encourage people to get out of the box—especially when they're setting goals—take the limits off, and *go for it,* the natural reaction is, *"But what if I go too far . . . what if I'm not being realistic?"*

Don't worry about it. Go ahead, dream big! Take the limits off. Set the goal. Write it down, and then write down the obstacles to getting there. And write down the action steps you'll take to get past the obstacles. *If the action steps you can realistically take cannot overcome the obstacles in front of you, the goal is too big.*

A goal of having, say, a million dollars in the bank six months from now—if you have nothing close to that at the moment—would obviously be unrealistic, because you wouldn't be able to come up with realistic action steps to overcome the obstacles.

Your action steps will always show you a clear picture of what it will take to reach the goal you've set. And because you'll always find out (with the action steps) if your goal is too big or not, that means you don't have to worry about reaching too far.

So imagine the best. *Dream big.* You can count on this rule to always keep your feet on the ground—even if your head is in the clouds.

Step #6 — Prioritize your "focus" goals.

Even if you set two or three goals in ten different key life areas (that would be twenty or thirty goals), you should still *focus* on only two or three of them at a time.

Prioritizing your goals is like saying to yourself, *"Which of my goals do I want to bring to the front this week? Which two or three goals do I want to keep in front of me, so I give them my attention, and make sure I do everything I need to do right now to reach them?"*

When you do that, it doesn't mean you ignore the rest of your goals—they're still there, and you're still aware of them, but you're choosing to give first place to the ones that are most important to give energy to right now.

There's a reason you should give this special kind of focus to only a very few goals at a time. It is because you have only so much energy to spread around at any one time. We've learned that as you increase the number of goals you're focusing on—beyond three of them at a time—your effectiveness goes down. So you have a better chance of reaching *more* of your goals, if each week you only focus on a few of them.

How do you do that? Just go through your goal list, read each of them, and ask yourself this question: *"If I could only concentrate on ONE goal this week, which one would I choose?"* Then check the one goal you would focus on. After that, ask yourself the same thing again, but this time choose a second focus goal. After that, choose a third. Stop there.

Remember, you can change your focus goals at any time. Every day if you'd like—though you probably wouldn't do it that often.

But the point is, by choosing three goals to focus on each week, you're telling yourself what's most important to work on at that moment. You're not stopping the other goals or ignoring them. They're still important. You're still working on them. But for the moment, they're just not at the very top of your list.

Step #7 — Review and track your goal plan on a schedule (preferably weekly).

Even though this is the easiest goal step of all, until you

develop the habit of doing it, you could find it difficult to commit the time—even the few minutes it actually takes—to reviewing your goals every week. I encourage you to make sure you take this step, every week, and make it a habit.

If you were being personally coached right now, your coach would help you make absolutely certain that you followed this step. And you'd want to send your coach a *Thank You* card, and maybe a dozen roses, when you saw the results you were getting.

Make this step a goal in itself. Write it out: *"To review and track my goals every week."* If you make the choice and the commitment to do this one thing, you'll make positive changes and create benefits in your life that will seem like magic or miracles. It won't be magic, of course; it will be *you*, putting yourself in control of your life.

THIS IS THE TIME TO UPDATE YOUR GOALS AND CHANGE THEM AS NECESSARY

Your weekly review is also the time to update your goals and action steps. Look at what's working and what isn't. Revise dates, and change the direction of a goal if you have to.

The analogy of the captain of a small ship—standing at the wheel and steering a course through the waves, avoiding the squalls of a storm in the distance—is an accurate picture of you. In your life, instead of manning the wheel of a ship, you might be sitting down with a cup of coffee and reading your goals early on a Monday morning. But the picture is the same. You're setting your course, getting through the day and the week, avoiding the storms, and steering for the sunlight and the smoothest water ahead.

Step #8—Reward yourself when you reach the goal—and reward yourself along the way.

Most of us were not taught to reward ourselves for our own accomplishments. Often, our parents were conditioned to believe it was bad manners to "brag" about a success, and they passed that program on to us. We were supposed to wait until someone *else* decided to reward us. So this is one step you may have to practice until you get it right.

I had to teach myself, as an adult, how to accept a reward— especially from *myself* for something I had done. I had grown up believing that rewards were for others, and our own accomplishments should be hushed in the self-imposed silence of humility. So the first time I ever gave myself a simple gift—just for accomplishing something I was proud of—I realized that this was something I would have to work to get used to. Happily, I have.

A POWERFUL KIND OF MOTIVATION

You might be surprised how effective even a small reward can be when you've completed a difficult action step or reached some important benchmark on the way to a goal. I've often done that myself and found it to be a powerful motivation. Even while *writing* about goals and motivation, I've found that rewarding myself really does help keep me motivated when it comes to finishing a difficult section of a book, or even completing a chapter.

Imagine how much fun you can have trying out rewards on yourself. Your self-rewards can be anything you like— *movies, dinners, spare time for yourself, clothes, toys and gadgets, a trip somewhere, a massage, a long phone call to an old friend, a book you've been putting off buying, a new car* . . . . Your reward can be anything you can imagine that you'd like to have and that you can afford to give yourself—but that you would otherwise probably *not* give yourself. (What is something you could give to yourself that you would really like to have?)

GIVING YOURSELF A GIFT—
AND A WHOLE LOT MORE!

Plan your rewards in advance. Easily and often say to yourself, *"When I get this done, I'm going to reward myself with . . . "* and then fill in the blank. Make it anything you'd like that you can give yourself. And when you reach the target—*give yourself the reward.* (Remember how you felt when a parent or someone else promised you something and then didn't come through on the promise? When you say you're going to give yourself a reward, do it.)

A final point to remember on self-rewards is that you should not rely on the completion of the goal itself to be its

own reward. The accomplishment you've wo
may well be rewarding in itself. But *all* of us can use a pa
the back and some well-deserved *"Congratulations!"* now
and then, along the way—even if it comes from us.

You should plan, right now, even if you haven't often
done this in the past, to reward yourself. There are few things
you can do that are healthier. When you take the time to
reward yourself, you're actually doing a whole lot more.
You're giving yourself more motivation to keep going; you're
encouraging yourself to recognize that you're making
progress; you're letting yourself know you believe in yourself
and you care about you; you're giving an important boost to
your self-esteem—*and* you get to enjoy the reward! All of
that comes from a simple reward that you give to *you*.

(Now then . . . how are *you* going to reward your*self* when
you finish this book? Think of something good.)

A FINAL REVIEW

As a quick overview, here are the eight steps for *"Active
Goal-Setting"* so you can review them easily at any time.

Step #1 — Identify the goal.

Step #2 — Write it down.

*Step #3 — Write down the date you're going to reach
the goal.*

128

Step #4 — List the obstacles to reaching the goal.

Step #5 — After each obstacle, write and date the action steps you're going to take.

Step #6 — Prioritize your "focus" goals.

Step #7 — Review and track your goal plan on a schedule (preferably weekly).

Step #8—Reward yourself when you reach the goal— and reward yourself along the way.

As you can see, none of the steps is difficult. They're just steps. But if you want to help yourself set goals and get them right, those are the right steps to take.

Chapter Twelve

It's Time for You

When you follow the steps and set goals for yourself (which we're going to do), I think you'll like what you find—especially when you read some of the goals you choose for yourself.

Even if you've set goals in the past, I believe you'll find the method we're applying here easier to use. By simply "filling in the blanks," you can set a goal—of any kind—and end up with a complete action plan *in just minutes*.

There are different areas of your life to consider when you're setting goals. It works best to set goals in each of the areas—to help you make sure your goals are well-rounded and your life is balanced. I'm going to give you the opportunity to look at each of these areas and to begin setting practice goals in any of them you choose—or in all of them.

ey goal areas we'll cover are:

1. *Lifestyle*

2. *Self-Esteem*

3. *Personal Organization and Control*

4. *Health and Fitness*

5. *Job and Career*

6. *Personal Relationships*

7. *Money and Finances*

8. *Personal Growth*

9. *Quality of Life*

10. *Other*

To show you how it works, I'll use an example of a goal in the area I call *"Lifestyle"* goals. Lifestyle goals could include anything that is part of your environment or how you live your life—everything from how and where you spend your free time, to the car you drive, the books you read, what you watch on television, where you go on vacation, the home you live in, the clothes you wear, who your friends are, your hobbies or avocation, or your daily routine.

As an example, we'll use Caroline, who wanted to ride

and work with horses—something she had enjoyed immensely when she was younger but hadn't been able to do for many years. Horseback riding had been on her *"I wish I could . . ."* list in the back of her mind, but she hadn't really figured out what to do about it.

Every time Caroline drove her teenage daughter to her friend's house, and they passed by homes with horse stables in the back yards, she thought about riding. Then, on her birthday, she realized time was flying by, and if she ever wanted to ride, she'd better do something about it.

Caroline's first step was to identify the goal, which she did. Next, she wrote out the goal: *"To go horseback riding and spend some time with horses at least once each month."*

Following the steps, she then wrote out each of the obstacles that could keep her from reaching the goal. She listed the problem of not having a public riding stable anywhere nearby, already having a busy schedule with too much to do, and wanting to spend more time just being with horses but not having a place to keep a horse of her own.

Once she had the obstacles identified and written down, Caroline went to work on the action steps—she wrote down what she would do to overcome each of the obstacles. Her action steps included finding out where the closest horses were kept, making a list of things in her busy schedule that were not important and could be dropped, and making a list of possible ways to have a horse of her own, or a horse that she could groom and personally take care of.

Her goal plan looked like this:

A. My goal is: *To go horseback riding and spend some time with horses at least once each month.*

B. The date I will reach my goal is: November 15 (and the year).

C. The obstacles to reaching my goal are:
   1. *There are no riding stables close by.*
   2. *My schedule is too busy already.*
   3. *Our property restrictions won't allow me to keep a horse at home.*

D. The action steps I will take to reach my goal are:
   1. *Research the area and find out where the closest horses are boarded or kept. (date)*
   2. *Make a list of everything on my schedule that I do not have to be doing and decide which things to drop. (date)*
   3. *Make a list of ways I can either have a horse of my own or a horse that I can personally groom and take care of. (date)*

E.   I will review and track this goal: Weekly, every Sunday night.

It was a simple goal plan, but Caroline followed the steps exactly. Less than a month later, Caroline was working with horses—and riding them! Here's what happened.

Her goal plan got her to one day drive up to one of the homes on the way to her daughter's friend's house—one of the homes with horses and a beautiful stable in the back yard—knock on the door, and introduce herself. She told the woman who lived there about her love of horses and asked the lady if she needed any help grooming hers.

Caroline had thought at first it might seem like an unusual question, so she was a bit uncomfortable asking. But as it turned out, the lady was delighted to have her help! A week later Caroline was helping groom the horses, and once each week she and the woman who owned the horses went riding for two hours to exercise them.

What Caroline had thought might be an impossibility only weeks earlier changed entirely—because she took a few minutes, gave the problem some thought, wrote out a goal plan, and then took the initiative to follow her simple plan.

THE PROCESS WRITES YOUR GOAL PLAN *FOR* YOU

It should be easy by now to see how the process works. It's a very simple process, and that's one of the reasons it works so well and why I recommend it. When you write out your own goals using these same steps, you don't have to spend a lot of time trying to figure out a goal plan—the process writes your goal plan *for* you.

As one other example, let's look at someone I met at a goal-setting seminar who surprised himself by setting a new career goal, and ended up changing his life. The young man named Casey, worked in computer drafting, but he found that even though the industry was still growing, his opportunities weren't. He considered himself a "motivated" individual, and he had read a number of self-help and personal improvement books. (He had set goals, but only passively; so far he had only written down his goals as a list, usually on his birthday.)

Casey was good at his work, but he knew he had other talents; he was intuitive and very good with people, talents that weren't being expressed at all in the cyber-environment of his computer drafting job. Even so, most of his goals were about improving himself as a draftsman or getting into management in drafting.

During the seminar that Casey attended on goal-setting, he participated in an exercise in which I asked all of the attendees to write out their "dream list"—what they would do with their lives if they could "wave their wands" and do anything they chose.

What Casey discovered was that "drafting" and "managing" were *nowhere* on his list. With that in mind, when he was asked to write out a specific goal and a goal plan to do what he really *wanted* to do, Casey surprised himself when he wrote out a sample goal plan—*in a completely different career.*

What Casey found himself writing as a goal had nothing at all to do with computers or drafting. It had to do with a picture of himself he had carried in the back of his mind for years—but believed he would never be able to bring to life. Casey wanted to work with people! Here's what he wrote:

A. ***My goal is***: *To have a high-opportunity job in career counseling.*

B. ***The date I will reach my goal is:*** March 15th (and the year—which Casey set as one year from the day he wrote out the goal).

C. The obstacles to reaching my goal are:
   1. I don't know what I would have to study to work in career counseling.
   2. I would have to take some classes, probably at night, and I'm not sure if I have the time to do that.
   3. I'm not sure if Jan (wife) will support me on this or not.
   4. I've never done anything like this before. I've always worked in drafting.

D. The action steps I will take to reach my goal are:
   1. Find out everything I can about career counseling and related fields. To do this I will:
       a. Go to the library. (date)
       b. Do research on the Internet. (date)
       c. Set up lunch meeting with Leonard (friend who works at an executive search firm). (date)
   2. Adjust my schedule to make this work. Use my computer schedule planner to do this. (date)
   3. Go out to dinner with Jan and talk with her. Let her know I'm willing to sacrifice to do this, but I will be keeping my current job meanwhile. Ask for her support. (date)
   4. Start immediately building my confidence and my self-esteem. Read or reread three good self-help books. (date)

E. I will review and track this goal: Weekly. Every Saturday morning.

What's remarkable about Casey's goal is that he first

wrote it down sitting in a goal-setting seminar with about 250 other people. When he arrived at the seminar that day, he had no idea that he would be setting a new goal that would change his life—certainly his career—for the better. (Or, at least, he was not *consciously* aware that's what he would be doing.)

Casey reached his goal—he did change careers. And even though it took him slightly longer than the one year he had scheduled for the shift, he thanks himself every day for writing out the goal—and this time getting it right. Writing that one, simple goal plan changed the rest of Casey's life.

WRITING YOUR STORY FOR YOURSELF

Every goal plan you might read, and its result, is a story in itself. What has impressed me as I've witnessed these stories in many people's lives is that for each of them, the story really starts *with the writing of the goal*. There may have been years of background that preceded the story, but the *action* begins with the setting of the goal. It's entirely possible that, as you write down your goals, you will be writing the first words of the story of the next years of *your* life.

Like Casey, many people surprise themselves when they read the goals they begin to write down. It's as if the mere physical act of writing down what we want unbinds our belief and unleashes the positive force of possibilities within us.

I hope that's true of you, with every goal you set.

Chapter Thirteen

Ten Goals That Can Change Your Life

If you set even one goal in each of the following ten goal areas, it's almost certain that your life will change—for the better. I'll go through the ten key areas with you and give you examples of the kinds of goals people set in each of them, so you'll have a picture of what your own goals in each area might be.

There's a reason people who do the best at setting goals set them in *all* of the 10 key areas—*lifestyle, self-esteem, personal organization, health and fitness, relationships, money and finances, job and career, personal growth, quality of life,* and *others*. It's because in our lives, our goals are all woven *together*.

Your self-esteem affects your job. Your job affects your finances. Your finances affect your relationships. Your relationships can affect your health and fitness. Your health and fitness affects the quality of your life. The quality of your life affects your personal growth. Which affects your self-esteem . . . and so on.

No goal that you set stands alone, independent of the rest of the things that are going on in your life. And it only makes sense that each goal you set—and the action steps that follow—should be consistent with the other goals you're setting, so they all work together.

The result of setting goals that work in harmony with each other is a kind of positive synergy; each action step you take in the pursuit of one goal works in concert with the steps you're taking in each of your other goals.

FINDING OUT WHAT YOU WANT

It's when you take the time to examine your goals in each of the key life areas that you begin to figure out what you really want. We're going to practice doing that now.

You'll find, as you think about which goals you'd like to set in each of the areas, that many of them can overlap. A goal to get more sleep, as an example, could be a health and fitness goal, but it could also be a lifestyle goal. A goal to take classes in a new subject may be a personal growth goal, but it could also be a job or career goal. Just write the goal in the area in which it most directly applies.

139

To make it easy to write out your goals, you can now go online to a Website that's designed specifically for *"active goal-setting"*—following the same steps we're using here—and print out blank goal-setting forms to use with each of the goal areas we're covering.

You can also set your goals directly online and write in your goals, obstacles, and action steps—you just fill in the blanks—in your own personal goal pages. When you do that you receive an E-mail every week, reminding you of your specific action steps for that week, along with some great motivation to stay with it. You can also print out your action plan so you have it in front of you throughout the week. (The Web address is *www.goals-on-line.com.*)

1. Your Lifestyle

Start by thinking of something in your "lifestyle" you would like to *add, improve,* or *change.*

It could be anything—how you spend your time, something about your home, something you'd like to do—anything that could be important to you.

Examples of lifestyle goals that people have set are:
To purchase a new automobile
To send our son and daughter to college
To build a house
To join the tennis club
To host a family reunion
To relax with a book at least two hours a week
To buy a home entertainment center

To plant a garden
To take ballroom dance classes
To paint the house
To travel
To get up thirty minutes earlier every morning
To go to bed thirty minutes earlier
To eat meals together as a family
To sleep in on Saturdays
To learn to SCUBA dive
To update my wardrobe
To take a vacation
To play the cello
To call home every week
To remodel and build a workout room in the attic
To cut television watching time by half

Did you find any goal ideas similar to your own on that list? When you think about your own lifestyle goals, keep in mind that they could be something you'd like to have accomplished weeks or months from now, or something you'd like to do sooner than that. Think about this question and answer it to yourself:

Is there anything in your lifestyle—how you live your life, or the environment you live in, that you'd like to change or improve in any way?

If there is something in your lifestyle you would like to change or improve, what is it? Then, just as though you were going to write out a goal plan, read each of the steps below and, for now, mentally fill in the blanks. First, what is the goal you're going to choose? Just think, *"What is my goal?"* If you need to, stop reading for a moment, sit back, and think about it. If you could add or change one thing in your lifestyle, what would it be?

A. *My (lifestyle) goal is:*
To _____

Then, write in the date you want to have achieved that goal. Write in a specific date—day, month, and year.

B. *The date I will reach my goal is* _____
(or, *I will see noticeable progress by* _____)

Now, think about any obstacle that could stand in the way, or anything you have to overcome or deal with in order to reach the goal. Repeat the specific goal to yourself that you just identified above. Then ask yourself, *"What obstacles do I need to deal with in order to reach this goal?"* Your next step will be to write each obstacle down just as you think it. (You may have more—or fewer—than three.)

C. *The obstacles to reaching this goal are*
    1. _____
    2. _____
    3. _____

Next, what do you have to do in order to deal with each of the obstacles? Come up with your best solutions, write them down, and write in the date you'll take that action. If you don't know what action to take to deal with one of the obstacles, then write in *"Research and find the best action step to take."* That, then, becomes an action step in itself—and gives you a specific time in which to come up with a solution. Write in as many (or as few) action steps as you need to get the job done.

D. *The action steps I will take to reach this goal are*
1. _____*(date)*
2. _____*(date)*
3. _____*(date)*

And finally, decide how often you're going to review this goal, check your progress, and make any changes you have to make. Far-off, long-range goals should be reviewed monthly. Near-term and short-term goals should be reviewed, or at least read, weekly—some of them daily.

E. *I will review and track this goal* _____

When you're actually setting the goal, of course, you would *always* write it out. As we've seen, a goal that is not written down has not been imprinted in your subconscious mind strongly enough—and you aren't likely to work hard to achieve it. If you write it down, there is a good chance that you *will*.

FILL IN THE BLANKS— AND CHANGE YOUR *LIFE*

It's astonishing how the simple step of writing a few words on paper can change your life in surprising and positive ways. When I first saw this happen in my own life, I didn't yet fully understand the immense capability of the subconscious mind to tirelessly seek the goal, and work at its completion (even when we're not *consciously* aware of what our own computer brain is doing for us). We type in the instructions—and we get the results.

If your own mind will do that, unconsciously, almost completely on its own, imagine what your mind will do if you give it some help! Every time you review your goal, every time you consciously take an action step, every time you even *think* about reaching that goal, you are combining forces with your goal-directed subconscious mind, creating an almost unstoppable team! *That* is how people reach their goals.

Now let's look at the other important goal areas and give you a chance to see what kinds of goals you'd like to set in each of them.

2. Your Self-Esteem

This is an important goal category, but it's one that some people overlook. If I were coaching you personally, I would recommend that you pay special attention to this area, and make sure that when you review your goals, you set at least one or two self-esteem goals. These are the goals that cover your self-confidence, your overall belief in yourself (*very* important to the process of goal achievement), how you think about yourself, how high you believe you should reach, and what you believe you can achieve in your life.

Examples of self-esteem goals that people have set are:
To write something positive about myself daily in my journal
To finish my college degree
To have a make-over
To spend time with people who make me feel good about myself
To listen every day to Self-Talk for building self-esteem
To lose 25 pounds in a healthy way
To always finish what I start
To reward myself when I do something I'm proud of
To do something for other people that helps them build their self-esteem
To set goals and work at reaching them

If you were to think about the makeup of your own self-esteem, is there anything you would *change* or *add* or *improve*? Think about that. Think about you, and how you feel about you—what you think about you. Are you the way you'd most like to be? If you could do one thing to improve your self-esteem, what would it be?

Once again, just start with the word, *"To . . ."*

A. My (self-esteem) goal is:
*To*_____

B. The date I will reach this goal is _____

C. The obstacles to reaching this goal are
    1. _____
    2. _____

     3. _____

D. *The action steps I will take to reach this goal are*
    1. _____*(date)*
    2. _____*(date)*
    3. _____*(date)*

E. *I will review and track this goal* _____

SAMPLE GOALS TO HELP YOU GET STARTED

Now, as we continue through the remaining goal areas, I'll give you a few sample goals in each of them to help you get started. (These are "thought starter" ideas that you can apply to your own goals. Mark this chapter and come back to it anytime you're working on setting a goal and you need some new ideas or input.)

3. *Your Personal Organization—and Being in Control of Your Life*

This is one goal area that people talk about a lot but may never get around to setting a goal about. They may *say* they've set a goal to get more organized, but their current state of disarray keeps them from doing anything about it. (Getting more organized is also a popular New Year's resolution—which also usually does nothing to solve the problem, unless you write out an actual goal and a goal plan which help you make your resolution a reality.)

The second part of this goal area—being in control of your life—is similar to being organized, but it expands the concept to putting you in charge, not just of your schedule and how organized your desk is, but also of what goes on in your life.

Sample goals for personal organization and control might include:

To get up one hour earlier each weekday
To schedule at least twenty minutes a day just for myself
To learn to say "no" and never over-commit
To never hit the snooze button on my alarm clock
To find a personal organizer that works for me and carry it with me at all times
To always keep my word when I say I'm going to be somewhere
To make a priority list of things I have to do each day
To organize my work space at home
To spend more time with other people who have a lot of personal organization and control in their lives.

Is there anything in your life you'd like to get more organized? Do you spend your time in a way that leaves you feeling good at the end of the day—instead of feeling like you're letting things go or leaving something undone? Do you say *"Yes,"* when you know it's better *not* to agree to do something? Do you feel in control of your life? Getting there starts with something as simple—but as powerful—as putting your goal into words—writing it down.

My goal for my personal organization and control is:
To _____

It's not my intention that you write out each of your goal plans here in the book. But by now, you have the process—you know what to do next. In each goal area, after you have an idea of the goal you'd like to work on (and you can have more than one in each area), write it down on paper, or go online to the active goal-setting site and print out the blank forms or write your goals online. Either way, take the time to fill in the blanks.

For now, think of at least one goal you might have in each of the areas. Don't worry about how it sounds, or whether it's too big or too small.

An important part of this practice is to get your mind to see yourself as a goal-setter. It's like the Self-Talk that says, *"I set goals and I reach them!"* With practice, and the right Self-Talk, the self-direction *"I set goals and I reach them,"* becomes *part* of you. When that happens, you begin to automatically look at the world around you—and your own self—in a profoundly different way. You start to see things in terms of possible goals instead of random wishes. You begin to think, *"I could do that . . . I could achieve that . . . I could be like that . . . I think I'll set a goal about it!"*

4. *Your Health and Fitness*

This is one of the most popular goal-setting areas of all. (If you've ever struggled with taking off a few pounds—and keeping them off—I don't have to tell you why.) It doesn't make much difference whether it's ten pounds or fifty, if your clothes don't fit, the angst and the anxiety deplete your energy and sap your self-esteem. Especially when it seems like nothing works. So it stands to reason that we would set goals to get our weight where we want it, and then keep it that way. But most people who want to lose weight have only a *target* and a *diet*— and that's it. No plan other than that.

I mentioned earlier that with the help of listening to recorded Self-Talk, I lost the fifty-eight pounds I had been fighting, and the weight never came back. Along with the Self-Talk I played in the background each day, I had a very clear goal plan—one that I wrote out, with obstacles and action steps, just as we're doing here. So I was able to track my plan faithfully every week. It was the combination of the recorded Self-Talk messages, along with a written goal plan, that made it work.

Of course, there are many other health and fitness goals that are not about weight or weight control. Running, exercising, working out, diet control and nutrition, relaxation and stress reduction, and general health—these are all pursuits that lend themselves especially well to setting goals.

Examples of health and fitness goals that people have set are:

To exercise a minimum of twenty minutes, four days a week

To stop drinking drinks with caffeine

To fit comfortably into a size 10 as my consistent size

To get a complete physical

To always take my medication on schedule, and never miss taking it

To stop smoking
To keep my cholesterol count below _____
To cut down fast-food lunches to no more than two times
a week
To get on a program to lower my blood pressure
To walk a minimum of one mile every morning before I
leave for work
To earn my next belt in Taekwondo
To lower my stress by meditating for twenty minutes each
day

Is there anything you'd like to do for your own health or fitness now that ought to be high on your goal list? If you closed your eyes and imagined a realistic picture of yourself being, physically, exactly the way you'd most like to be, what would that look like? Get a good picture of a health and fitness goal you'd like to reach.

My goal for my health and fitness is:
To_____

5. *Your Job and Career*

Examples of job and career goals would include:
To find five new clients each month
To find a different career from the one I'm now in
To reach a sales goal of _____
To write a schedule for my daily activities
To stop taking work home on weekends

To attend night school
To find a way to work only part time
To get the help of a business coach
To always get my reports done on time
To avoid participating in company gossip and politics
To write an actual plan for my advancement
To find a business that I can operate from my home
To get my promotion

What is one thing about your job or your career that you would like to change or improve?

My goal for my job and career is:
*To*_____

6. Your Relationships

It's curious that many people either take the success of their relationships for granted, or accept them as part of fate—as though they were scripted by someone else. Good relationships work, when we work *at* them. And the secret to that is setting goals—which lets *you* write at least part of the script.

Examples of relationship goals are:
To develop better communication with our kids
To meet the girls for lunch at least once a week
To practice following the golden rule
To patch things up with _____ and be friends again
To stop giving advice

To bring flowers home to my wife at least twice a month
To become a better listener
To never lose my temper
To spend more time with me, *enjoying who I am*
To stop arguing completely
To be more positive

If you were to write down one goal to change or improve a relationship that is important to you, what would it be?

My personal relationships goal is:
*To*_____

7. *Your Money and Finances*

This is a popular goal area for goal-setting, and it lends itself to setting very specific goals.

Examples of goals for money and finances could include:
To increase my income to $_____ per month
To write out a budget and follow it
To pay off my credit card balances every month
To save $24,000 for the down payment on the house
To develop a ten-year financial strategy
To give $150 to the children's charity every month
To create an actual plan to pay for the kids' college tuition
To take a course on investing
To review my insurance policies and get all of them brought up to date

To increase my income by 20% this year
To be able to work part time with no strain on the budget
To refinance the house to get a lower interest rate

Think about your own finances. What is it you want? What would you do if you could wave your wand and create the financial position that would be both practical and perfect for you? If you were to set one goal about your money and finances, right now, what would it be?

My goal for my money and finances is:
To _____

If you're getting a picture of a goal you could set that would help you, take the few minutes it takes to fill out a goal sheet and fill in all of the blanks. Then read it over. You'll feel great about yourself for taking a first step, and you'll have the beginning of a new plan that could make a *real* difference in your financial well-being.

8. *Your Personal Growth*

I place personal growth goals high on any list of goals. That may be because that's the field I work in; yet, in the most practical sense, it's easy to recognize that *everything* we do stems from who we are—*and who's steering our ship.* The example of the computer has been often used—"your *output* is equal to your *input*." And it's true. You will *get* from yourself in direct proportion to what you *give* to yourself.

If you keep learning new things, think often and deeply, keep a youthful sense of curiosity and a strong determination to get better every day, then the results of your efforts are going to show in everything you do.

Who are you as an individual? How is your thinking? How is your wisdom? How much do you know? How much more do you think you'll learn? *How much more can you grow?*

Some examples of goals that people have set for their personal growth are:

To read at least one biography of an exceptional person each month this year

To make a list of three people I admire and would like to know, and get to know them

To set goals in each of the goal-setting areas and track them every week

To make a list of the ways I'd like to improve myself in the next five years, and focus on them one at a time

To get my degree in _____

To meditate at least three times a week

To take a vocabulary CD course

To do something to benefit me that I'm afraid to do

To travel to a place I've never been before

To donate one day of my time each month to charity

To do something each day to help someone else

That could be a very long list. There is so much we can do to get better. Most of it even costs very little. We just have to make it important to us, and we have to make the choice to do it.

If you could do one thing right now to improve yourself, what would it be?

My goal for my personal growth is:
To _____

9. Your Quality of Life

How is the quality of your life *overall*? As a way to measure, ask yourself how you feel when you lay your head down on the pillow at night, and how you feel when you first wake up in the morning.

Your quality of life is how things are working for you, how "happy" you are, or how fulfilled, and how at peace you are with yourself and your life right now. This isn't looking for perfection in an imperfect world; it's more about creating the greatest quality of life each day that you can. And since, ultimately, it does seem to be the *quality* of our life that most of us are working to improve, it would make sense for you to look at your quality of *your* life, ask some good questions, and then set some practical goals to improve those things that don't yet measure up to what you want.

Some examples of goals for the quality of life might include:
To find a hobby I really enjoy
To spend more time with my family on weekends
To keep my space and my time better organized so I have the time and place to do more things I enjoy
To listen to more classical music— especially Vivaldi and

Mozart
To get my vision corrected with laser procedure so I don't
have to wear glasses anymore
To talk to my father more often
To turn off (or unplug) the television
To go on a drive to nowhere in particular
To do more reading just to relax
To work to reach each of the other goals I'm setting
To go to church
To count my blessings and be thankful for them every
night before I go to sleep

How *is* your peace of mind? Is there anything you can do about that? How happy are you? How many times a day do you smile? How often do you sit back, take a deep breath, look at your day, or the moment, and feel really *contented* —happy with your life?

The great blessing is that we have been given the gift of personal choice—and each of us is given the power to create immense quality in our lives. Peace of mind. Joy. Deep satisfaction. Enthusiasm. Positive expectation. Each of these is ours to create, but we have to *choose* to have it.

Rather than waiting for "someday," when things will be bright and happy and life is working, look at it from a more actualizing point of view: *you're in control of the quality of your life.* You're in control of your attitude and everything you think. Or, at least, you're in control the moment you decide to *take* control.

That right is your gift. You were given that at birth. And even though it may have taken many years and a lot of lessons to get you to where you are today, now might be a good time to accept the gift. Take control. Decide *exactly* what you want for the quality of your life.

> *My goal for my quality of life is:*
> *To* _____

10. Your "Other" Goals

And finally, there is a place for the goals that don't easily fit anywhere else. These goals may benefit us in other ways, but the real reason for working on them is because we want to, or feel personally compelled to. When Judith Ann wanted to learn to play the guitar, it wasn't so she could play in a band or even perform for the family; she just wanted to play the guitar. She didn't even do it for "personal growth." She just wanted to make some music on a guitar.

There are many goals that don't seem to fit one of the other, more clearly defined categories. When you think of a goal like that, just go to the category of "Other" and write out the goal.

Here are a few examples to give you ideas of what "other" goals might look like:
> *To learn to fly an airplane and get my pilot's license*
> *To become proficient at using photo and graphics programs on my computer*
> *To do volunteer work at the hospital*
> *To do a complete genealogy study of my family tree*
> *To take piano lessons*
> *To join Toastmasters and learn to be comfortable speak-*

ing in front of a group
To join an amateur astronomy group
To get some clay and make a sculpture
To build a wood-working shop in the garage
To write a book and get it published

If you were to write down one of these "other" goals, what would it be?

My other goal is:
*To*_____

A SCRIPT, A ROAD MAP, AND A WAND

Those ten areas of goals give you a script, a road map, and a wand. The script is the *future* that you have the privilege to write for yourself. The road map is the *plan* to follow, so you'll know how to get there. And the wand is the magic of imagination—being able to see your own future, and then make it come true.

That's what this breakthrough—*active* goal setting—learning to set goals in the right way, will do for you. What an incredible, life-changing gift we've been given! I hope you'll use the gift.

PART THREE

Your Help & Support

"All self-help
works better when
you have *help*.

If you want to
do your best,
get the right help."

Chapter Fourteen

Getting the Help You Need

Now we come to the third ingredient of the formula that brings together the *best* of the tools for personal growth. This important part of the formula, personal (or business) coaching, helps you reach new heights—with *help* at your side.

If you had the right <u>help</u>, imagine what you could do.

With the help of a professionally trained coach, I've seen people build their careers or their businesses to successes they had only dreamed of. I've watched people become financially safe and strong for the first time *ever*—even wealthy. I've seen people get awesomely fit, lose weight and keep it off, improve their marriages, get their lives organized, or awaken to a whole new world of possibilities and successes—all because they found this one concept, personal coaching, and put it into practice in their lives.

FINDING WHAT'S BEEN MISSING

As I studied the important fields of human behavior and motivational psychology, it became clear to me that many people who wanted to do better would make greater strides if they had some *help*. (Some people even needed help just getting *started*.)

As a result of my research, I had learned how, with the right Self-Talk, we could change our old programs that had been working against us. We had also learned how to set goals in an active new way—and have an actual plan to follow.

But as I watched people work at getting better, I saw, again and again, that for many of them there was an inertia, an invisible wall that held them back. They knew the problem. They could *see* the solution in front of them. But it was almost as though they were powerless to do anything about it.

I watched people in seminars who clearly experienced breakthroughs. You could see they had figured it out! They *knew* that all they had to do was change their programs and set the right goals, and they could reach any star on their horizon. And yet, many of those same, deserving people would return to their homes and to their jobs, settle back into a world of perpetual inaction (or frustration)—and do *nothing*.

There were those who worked at making changes and had *some* success—but yet, there was still something missing.

161

Something that their own internal resources, by themselves, weren't giving them. The obvious solutions were there, but even though these people wanted to improve themselves, and knew the answers, they weren't putting the solutions into practice.

Something was missing.

SOMETHING THAT WOULD ALMOST *GUARANTEE* SUCCESS

The answer to the problem brought me full circle. I said earlier that I had begun my journey through the world of personal growth many years ago as a personal life coach—helping people identify who they were and what they wanted and how to achieve it. It became clear to me that if someone wanted to find focus, set the right kind of goals, and have the highest possible chance of reaching them, then having a personal coach or the right business coach would almost *guarantee* more success.

Think about something important in your own life. Let's say that you really want to move forward in some way—in something that would help you as a person or would make a difference in your life. This could be anything that's important to you—your business, your fitness, your marriage, your family, your finances—anything at all. And let's say that up to now, even though it's been important to you, you haven't made the progress in that area you'd like to have made.

But now, instead of trying to do it by yourself, let's say you have *help*—you have a coach. Someone who knows about focus, and goals, and motivation, and keeping you moving. And your coach is 100% on *your* side. So the person helping you is noncritical and understanding. Your coach knows what you want, and is dedicated to helping you get it.

Now, every week or every two weeks, you have an incredible coaching session—a time that's all about you. Your coach is an expert in helping you discover the right areas of focus in your life, who you are and what you want, and what your goals should be and what to do about each of them.

So in each of those uplifting and enlightening sessions, your coach reviews your progress with you. Together the two of you go over your action steps, review what you've done during the previous days, and identify and lay out your goals and action steps for the days ahead. Meanwhile, your coach is encouraging and supportive, so now you also have the attitude and motivation you need to stay with it!

Because you have a coach, you also now have a point of *accountability*—your coach is never critical, but you still want to live up to your personal commitment to take the action steps you agree on each time you talk.

And it works! Day after day, week after week, with each action step, you move closer and closer to reaching each of your goals. And the one difference—the one that makes it work is that you have a coach.

Having a coach of that kind could benefit any of us. And with many of us, it could be the difference between actually making the right kinds of changes in our lives—or *not*.

THE DILEMMA

In recognizing that personal coaching was a key part of the solution, I also recognized a dilemma—and the more we could use the help of a coach, the bigger the dilemma becomes. Why? Because it is often precisely those people who could most *use* the help of coaching and do well with it, who are not aware that it's available, or don't know how to get it.

Some people who read this may not be familiar with this kind of coaching. Others, even if they've become familiar with the concept of personal coaching or business coaching, still have no idea how to get the right kind of coaching, or even what to look for.

And still others, including those who might benefit most from the help of a good coach, might automatically assume that coaching is a luxury—something *other* people get to have—but one they could never have for themselves. (Even if it were the coaching itself that might help them *solve* their problems with finances, they don't know that they could afford to have a coach—so they never consider having one.)

It was apparent to me that combining the help and support of the right kind of *coaching*—with the use of *Self-Talk* and *active goal-setting*—created an incredible combination for success. Self-Talk, active goal-setting, and personal coaching, used *together*, offered the most practical solution to personal achievement that I had found in thirty years of work in the field of human behavior.

164

I knew the concept of coaching was a *key* to the solution. So many times, as I saw people begin to break through—begin to change their programs, and start to create focus in their goals—I also saw that with outside help, support, encouragement, motivation—they would *really* break through! They would win! And they would make the kinds of changes in their lives that they had only dreamed of making.

So often, when I saw someone seeing his or her own potential for the first time, but struggling with how to get there, I was reminded again of the personal coaching program I had conducted years earlier, and the positive changes that had come from that experience in other people's lives.

I kept coming back to the successes I'd seen time and again, proving how life-changing coaching could be.

A CLASSIC CASE OF COACHING

As an example, one of my early coaching clients whom I'll never forget, a man named Curtis, had told me that even though he was working as a successful executive in the aerospace industry, his great love was classic automobiles, and he wanted to somehow spend time working with cars—a dream he knew he would never realize. Some time later, following the time Curtis had gone through the coaching program, I met him again by accident one day at a restaurant in another city. I hadn't seen him since he had gone through the coaching program five years earlier.

I heard my name being called across the restaurant, and there was Curtis. Very excited, he immediately jumped up and gave me a big hug, and then began introducing me to the friends he was with at his table. He had a sparkle in his eyes and he looked like he had never been happier. "This is the man I've been telling you about," Curtis said to them. "Shad is the guy who's responsible for us being here." Since the time I had last talked to him, unbeknownst to me, Curtis had become one of the top leaders in classic car auctions in the country, and was traveling throughout the United States, holding auctions, surrounded by his friends in the business—and those beautiful cars of his dreams.

Though he gave me credit for his being there, I had nothing to do with it other than helping Curtis figure out who he was *inside*, and what he really wanted to do with his life. Curtis did it himself. And it was easy, once the coaching helped him set the right goals and get on the right track.

EXPERIENCING COACHING
FOR YOURSELF

Time after time I had witnessed success stories of people like Curtis, and all those successes were the result of that one thing—each of them had gotten their lives or their businesses on track because, with coaching, they had *help*.

Later, as I began to research the important concepts of first Self-Talk and then Active Goal-Setting, and I no longer had the time to devote to individual coaching, I kept coming back to those people and what they had achieved as a result of of their coaching. I had met others of my past coaching clients, and one after another their stories were the same.

Like Curtis, each of them had found success—and a great deal *more*. I knew that virtually anyone could enjoy similar kinds of success if, in some way, they could experience coaching for themselves. It's a tool that today anyone *can* use—and *should*.

I spent a long time studying the problem: *If having a coach is that effective, then everyone ought to have one.* But how do you let everyone experience the exhilarating "wake up" and exciting new mind-set that coaching creates? (Before we're willing to try something new to us—like coaching— even if it could solve our biggest problems and change our lives forever, we have to have an idea what it will do for us.)

The answer is, of course, that ultimately the best way for you to know what coaching will do for you will be to experience it for yourself. That, you can't get from the reading of a book.

But I can, however, give you an understanding of *why* coaching works so well. In the following chapters I'm going to share two "stimulating" exercises with you. Each of them will help explain, in simple terms, the powerful psychological underpinnings that make coaching work, and why coaching affects people's lives in such a dramatic and positive way.

One of these exercises you can do by yourself, and the other you can do with your spouse or a friend. With each of these exercises, we'll begin to see that the real key to having an *outside* coach—is what happens *inside us*.

Chapter Fifteen

Turning Your "Success Switches" *ON!*

To begin to show you why coaching works so well, there is an exercise you can try immediately—by yourself.

Doing this simple exercise won't give you the benefits you'd get from working with your own personal coach, but it will give you some insight—and a sample of what lies ahead.

The exercise, a self Q&A, will, on the surface, help you find out if you're on track with where you want to be going —right now. But it also sets you up in another way— *internally*—for taking action and moving forward.

Here's how it works. A good coach is able to help us see ourselves—and even give us direction—by asking the right questions. So it makes sense that we would gain some of the same insight by asking those same kinds of questions of *ourselves*, and then *listening* to what we have to say. Answering the questions in this exercise will help you do that.

But this exercise also shows us what happens, *inside* us, when we have the right *input*—the right "stimulation" from an outside source. (The coach.) And this has to do with a physiological facet of the human brain: important parts of the brain are *designed* to be literally "turned on"—like turning on electrical switches—and stimulated to help us succeed.

This exercise will show you, even if in a limited way, (since you're doing it by yourself), what happens when you turn your *Success Switches "ON!"*

GETTING *"TUNED IN"* TO *YOU*

I mentioned earlier that, for several years, I've written a weekly and bi-weekly coaching letter called the *"Personal Life Coach Letter,"* which I send by E-mail to thousands of people all over the world. Some time ago, in the letters I sent out, I began writing questions for my readers to ask themselves as a self Q&A exercise—much like the one I've included here. I knew how effective an exercise of this kind could be, but it surprised many of the people who tried it.

My readers wrote to tell me they were doing exactly as I had suggested; they were printing out the list of questions I had given them, and were then reading the questions and giving themselves their answers, sometimes out loud, and listening very carefully to the answers they gave.

The result was that when they answered the questions, they almost instantly became *"tuned in"* to themselves and where they were going. They were *more focused, more aware, more energized*—and they were suddenly ready to start setting goals and taking action. There's a reason for that.

CREATING MORE *"SUCCESS ACTIVITY"* IN YOUR BRAIN

When you answer the right kinds of questions—as in this exercise—or when you engage in the ongoing communication you have with a professional coach—you're actually stimulating vital areas of your brain, and creating a higher level of brain activity in an extremely positive way. What happens when you do this is based on a scientific principle of how energy is created in the brain, and it's a principle that is at the heart of personal coaching, and why coaching works so well.

This is how the process works:

The more you think about something, the more you concentrate on it, talk about it, study it, review it, take action on it, make it important, repeat it, make a habit of it—*or answer questions about it*—the more electrical and chemical activity you create in your brain. So you're actually flipping the *"Success Switches"* in your brain, and turning them *"On."* (*Negativity* and *inactivity* turn them *"Off."*)

Each time you go through a coaching session—and long after—you're flipping those switches to the *"On"* position and *increasing* the amount of chemical and electrical energy

170

and activity in your brain. And that new force of energy is directed entirely at *boosting your attitude, sharpening your thinking, focusing your attention, increasing your vision, and putting you into action.*

When you're asked certain kinds of questions about yourself, your mind *wants* to come up with the right answer. The brain is engineered that way.

Searching for the right answer, *your brain begins to turn itself on*—chemically and electrically. When you think about the question, and then concentrate on the answer, parts of your mind that frequently go unused begin to *wake up.* Chemical/electrical neural circuits come alive with activity! Your full mental capacity, *alerted by the question that was asked,* awakens from its slumbering state, snaps to attention and rises to the challenge. (It's no wonder that when you're being coached you feel more alert and alive! You *are.*)

THE Q&A EXERCISE

In our exercise here, when you answer the questions, notice what's really happening. What you're actually doing is turning some of those same switches *"On"* and chemically stimulating important neural pathways in your brain.

Those are the switches that control your focus, your attention, your attitude, and your actions—so you're putting more of the immense chemical and electrical energy of your own brain to work for you! When your brain is active and alive—so are you! (When a trained, professional coach is working with you, you'll be turning those switches *on* times ten—or a *hundred!* Imagine what happens when you're working with the right coach—and you're turning on *all* of the right switches!)

A SAMPLE LIST OF QUESTIONS

To give you an example of how it works, and to try a simple exercise of this kind for yourself, the only thing you need is a list of some of the right questions. To make it easier, I've written a simplified list of sample questions for you. (Since we've been working on goals, I've also focused the questions in this exercise on goals. The questions could have had to do with *anything* that's important to you or would help you move forward.)

I've also modified the questions I'm asking you in the exercise, to make it easier and more natural for you to ask these questions of yourself.

Read each of these questions as though you were actually asking them of yourself as an outside coach would ask them. (To do this right, and actually begin to create the positive increase in neural activity in your brain, since you're doing this by yourself without the aid of an outside coach, it's important that you give *extra* focus and attention to each question. You would do that automatically if someone else were asking you the questions—but here, creating that initial mental stimulation will be up to you. It will help if you *repeat* each question one or two times, thinking about it as you do, to make sure you're giving it your full concentration.)

Also, answer each question as though you were talking to the most important person in the world. (You are.)

As you answer each question, notice what happens when you become focused, begin to really think about your answers, and start to turn the chemical switches in your brain to the *"On"* position:

1. *How are you doing this week?*

2. *Do you feel you're "on target" and doing the right things? (Are you doing the things you'd <u>like</u> to be doing?)*

3. *Is there anything you should be doing that you're not now doing?*

4. *If there is any one thing that might be holding you back or getting in the way of you reaching your goals right now, what would it be?*

5. *What goals did you clearly identify to work on this past week?*

6. *How did you do on each of them?*

7. *Is there anything you wanted to accomplish in the past week that you did not accomplish?*

8. *What would you like to do about that?*

9. *Did you learn anything this past week that can help you reach any of your goals?*

10. *What goals would you like to focus on next?*

11. *What, if anything, is keeping you from reaching any of those goals?*

12. *What will you do to deal with the obstacles, to help you reach the goal?*

13. *How would you rate your attitude right now? (And why?)*

14. *How is your "focus"?*

15. *What is one thing you could do right now to get more focused, get on track, and get motivated?*

16. *What will you do about that?*

17. *How do you feel about yourself when you're accomplishing something you want to accomplish?*

18. *How do you feel about yourself right now?*

19. *What is one thing you could do in the next week that would help you move forward?*

20. *What will you do about that?*

21. Is there anything else you'd like to talk about that we haven't covered here?

When you take the time to focus on the questions, and think each of your answers through clearly, you're doing something that few of the people around you seldom (if ever), do—you're taking the time to focus entirely on you, and what's important to you.

If you went through the exercise in the way I suggested, there is no doubt that you increased both your brain activity and your awareness. Done in the right way, that simple exercise can get you to think, and even want to take some action.

Imagine then, what would happen if you could turn those same, healthy, positive switches to the *"On"* position, and keep the right ones turned on—not just for a few minutes, but every time you needed to take action and move forward. Doing that translates directly to setting more good goals, having a great attitude, feeling good about yourself, making positive changes, and getting things done!

That's one of the things an outside coach helps you do. And it's one of the reasons that good coaching is so effective; in all of my research, I've never found any other business or personal growth tool *that can turn the same switches "on" and help you keep them that way.*

That simple exercise gives you an idea of what lies ahead—and lets you know there's a lot more to come.

175

Chapter Sixteen

Another Step In
The Right Direction

This next exercise takes you another step closer to the very real idea of having a personal coach in your own life.

In this exercise you'll be sharing the Q&A session with a friend—just like the *self* Q&A exercise we discussed in the previous chapter, except this time someone else is going to be asking you the questions. (You'll do the same for that person at a different time, so both of you will benefit from the exercise.)

When someone else is asking the questions, your awareness level is heightened. You're more aware of the answers you're giving because you know someone else is listening to what you have to say. (Even if that other person doesn't add a single word in comment, you still know that person is there.)

So you may answer the same questions differently. Once again, you get the benefits from gaining insight into your own feelings, attitudes, and focus in much the same way as in the previous exercise, but now, to a greater degree.

When the questions are coming from someone else, psychologically they have more validity. This has to do with our conditioning—sitting in classrooms, responding to adults, and being talked to by the authority figures in our early lives. The person asking the questions is in a naturally authoritative role, so we "listen" to each question differently than if we were asking the same questions of ourselves. Even though we know we're going through a simple exercise, we take each question more seriously. We want our answers to make sense, to sound intelligent.

The fact that someone else is listening—*really* listening—also increases the emotional level of our responses; it's not often that someone really *listens* when we're expressing ourselves. Though we're not conducting therapy, a fact of our psychological makeup is that it is also "therapeutic" to be listened to. So that facet, too, is added when someone else is asking you the questions, and then listening to what you have to say.

TURNING EVEN *MORE* SWITCHES *ON*

The result of all this is, that when someone else asks the

questions, the dynamic changes. Even more of you is listening and responding. So in the brain, another whole section of your *"success switches"* is turned *on*. When that happens (as we saw in the previous chapter), more of your brain is awakened and brought to attention—stimulating your thinking and your responses, and, if they're the right questions, setting you up for greater action.

And that's the key to this exercise. Proving to ourselves in a simple twenty-minute exercise how, with the right input, the right *stimulus*—in this case a few of the right kind of questions—our brain will automatically and naturally *respond*. The basic response is to want to take action.

In other words, if you want to move ahead in your business or in your life in some way (and it's ultimately up to your mind, your *brain*, to take you there), if you can get the right kind of "input" (*stimulation* and *activation*), your brain will naturally and automatically give you the right kind of *output*. And with the kind of input you get from a business coach or a personal coach—that translates directly into *action*: finding your focus, setting and tracking your goals, taking action steps, staying motivated, and moving forward—reaching goal after goal after goal. And it all starts with the right *input*.

Once again, with this exercise, we're not attempting to take the place of a coach; that would be impossible to do. We're simply experiencing for ourselves what happens when we get even a small *sample* of the right kind of input, stimulation, questions, direction, response. All that comes, in our exercise, from the asking of a few questions.

THE EXERCISE

To give you a better idea of what's to come, try this exercise with someone you trust. Remember, however, even though you're going through this exercise with someone else, the exercise itself is designed to give *you* the experience of recognizing what happens *inside* when you're responding to the questions.

So the exercise really isn't about the other person. That person is there to facilitate the questioning and to make the exercise, to some degree, an interactive experience. The exercise is for *your* benefit. (To reciprocate, at a different time you'll take on the role of the person who asks the questions.)

In fact, it's essential that your friend—the person you choose to go through this exercise with you—not play any role other than that of asking the questions and letting you answer. No personal advice, no comments, no opinions, no point of view—just the questions. (Trained coaches know how to do that. Unfortunately, most friends do not.)

First, think of a friend who might like to go through the exercise with you, and discuss the idea with that person. (You may want to loan your friend your copy of this book and say, *"Here, read this. When you're done reading it, let's talk."*)

After you agree to work on this together, set a good time for that person to call you. Set up a *separate* time for you to call that person for his or her turn to be asked the questions.

It works best to separate the exercise periods in this way so that each of you will have better focus when it's your turn to answer the questions. Each of you should plan to spend about thirty minutes on the phone to go through the exercise.

GETTING STARTED

I recommend that each of you use the list of questions I wrote for you in the previous chapter. You may want to write out additional questions of your own, and also use other questions I've included in the book as a guide to follow.

You might think that going through the exercise in this way would be more fun and interesting if you did this in person, perhaps over coffee. Fun and interesting, yes. But helpful? No. This exercise should be done, if at all possible, by phone. Just like a trained professional coach would conduct a session with you on the phone, your friend should call you at the appointed time, say hello, get the pleasantries out of the way, and begin by asking the first question.

The rest of the exercise will follow, question by question. While your friend is asking you the questions in the exercise, he or she will be doing very little of the talking—in fact, almost none. You'll be listening to each question, and then answering each question as completely as you can. But you'll be listening especially carefully to what's going on *inside*, as you begin to see the picture that your answers create. (Listen *very* carefully, and you may be able to hear some of those switches being clicked into the *"On"* position.)

180

A FEW SIMPLE RULES

There are only a few things you'll need to do to make this exercise work effectively. The rules are simple, but important. These rules apply to each of you when you're the one asking the questions.

1. Be objective. See yourself in the role of the completely open, non-critical, supportive friend. Do your best to stay in that role throughout the entire exercise.

2. Just ask the questions, and let the other person talk. When they pause, or seem to come to the end of their answer, give them more time to think or to reflect on what they just said. Many times the person's *real* answer will come after they've listened to what they just said—and realize the real answer is something else. Make your most important asset your silence.

3. Don't give the other person your opinion, and don't give advice. There's a fine line between discussing ideas and options—and giving advice. When in doubt, ask the other person the question, "What do *you* think you should do?"

4. Don't allow yourself to get sidetracked. Know in advance what questions you're going to ask, and if the other person goes too far afield from the question, ask it again. If the other person answers the question, but forgets the

objective and loses focus, politely step in and ask the next question.

5. Always be encouraging. Let the other person know that you're confident in him or her. Be genuine about your encouragement, and mean it. If it's genuine, it will help.

GOING THROUGH THE EXERCISE
WITH YOUR SPOUSE OR YOUR MATE

To go through this exercise at home—especially with your spouse or mate, or someone close to you—you'll have to pay special attention to the rules I've listed above. (You also won't be using the telephone.)

The most important thing for you to remember is that when you're the one asking the questions, just ask the questions—and let your mate talk. Sit back, disconnect yourself if you have to, keep your opinions to yourself, and give your mate a chance to answer and a chance to listen to his or her own answers.

It might take some practice doing this, because it may be very different from the way the two of you are used to communicating with each other. But if you both understand why you're doing this, and how it works best, you should be able to step into the "role" and make the experience work for you.

Whether you go through this exercise with a friend, or try it at home with your spouse or mate, the key to the exercise is to begin to recognize what it feels like to *stimulate* and *activate* the natural success mechanism of the brain, and to put *it* into action—which will help put *you* into action.

Experiencing the results that even this simple exercise can create (you almost immediately start thinking about setting goals and taking some action), it's not difficult to recognize how much a trained *coach* is able to do—in a far greater way —to help you find your focus, set the right goals, put you into action, keep you on track, and keep you motivated and moving forward, day after day, week after week. *That's* when it gets exciting! That's when you start reaching every goal you set.

"COACHING" YOUR KIDS

I'd also like to recommend that you use the same concept we're using in this exercise, modify it and adapt it, and use it with your kids—but this time, for a very different reason.

When you and a friend are going through the exercise, you're getting a feel for what happens when the stimulus/ response nature of the exercise increases your level of self-awareness, with the added benefit that you find yourself wanting to make some choices and take some action. That, in turn, suggests to you what you could actually do if you had the help and support of an outside coach who worked with you on a far broader and more active level, goal after goal, month after month—and I hope you'll do that.

Unfortunately, as of yet there are only a very limited number of coaching programs for kids, and only one or two that come close to doing for children or teenagers what business or personal coaches now do for the rest of us. (If you'd like to get information on coaching programs that are available for kids, I've included a source on the *Resources* page at the back of the book.)

Kids at just about any age respond to good "coaching" concepts, including setting goals and reaching objectives (and getting rewards).

If you have young people in your life, consider taking the time to talk with them—but this time, instead of giving advice, practice a form of this exercise. Ask them the right kinds of questions, and watch what happens.

Instead of saying, as an example, *"I want you to study more,"* replace that discussion with questions such as: *"What kind of grades would you most like to make?" "What kind of student would you most like to be?" "What goal would you like to set for your grades?" "What is one thing you'd really like to do, as a reward, when you reach that goal?"* . . . and let them listen to their own answers. (Remember, in this case you're actually being their coach—let them do the talking.)

CHANGING THEIR FUTURES
BY COACHING THEM NOW

With some practice, you can get exciting results from holding actual coaching sessions with your kids—short, weekly sessions, but held on a regular schedule, say, fifteen or twenty minutes every Saturday morning. (If that schedule won't work in your household, try every two weeks or once a month. However often you do this, it's worth it.)

With each of your kids, go through a brief list of coaching questions, including how they did on the goals and action steps they set for the previous week—and which action steps they want to set for the week to come. Follow the same question-and-answer format every week, so they get used to it and know what to expect—and they begin to think about what they're going to say.

Using this concept, teenagers—and even very young children—can learn to set goals, track them, reach them, and achieve the rewards. Kids learn very quickly that if they can reach even *one* goal they set . . . they can reach *another*. And then *another*. And then *another*.

When you're talking with your kids, use the same principles we've been discussing throughout this book.

Help your kids with their *Self-Talk*, so they get their programs right, right from the start.

Help them with their *goals*, so they get into the habit of setting goals *now*, a habit that will benefit them for the rest of their lives.

And take the time to be their *life coach* in some way every day. Coach them now, so when they become grown, they won't need a personal coach to help them—they'll already have it figured out.

185

Chapter Seventeen

Having Your Own Coach

Now it's time to turn all of your switches to the "On!" position. It's time to move to the life-changing and fully inter-active experience of having a trained professional coach for yourself. If you're serious about your own success, having the help of a professional coach should be at the top of your list of tools.

The day we were expected to rely solely on ourselves to make forward progress in our lives is long gone. Today, if you wanted to get physically fit—and do really well at it—you would certainly benefit from the help of a qualified physical trainer. If you wanted to learn how to sell real estate in the best way, you'd go through training and have an experienced instructor to guide you. If you wanted to backpack through the Amazon, you wouldn't consider going without having a professional guide at your side.

Why would you do any *less* when you want to improve

yourself in some way, or get better in your business or in some other area of your life? If you wanted to do that, and do it well, it makes sense that you would get the help of a good coach—just like you would enlist the help of a trainer, an instructor, or a guide in anything else that called for it.

WHAT WILL YOUR
PROGRAMS TELL YOU?

Before you think you could never have a coach for yourself, consider this: professional coaching is a tool that today is so worthwhile and so accessible that there are literally thousands of people being coached right now.

I know that when we think about something that may be out of the "ordinary"—even if it's something incredibly worthwhile, like being coached—our own past programs might try to make us think we somehow don't qualify—no matter how helpful coaching might be. Our old programs tell us, *"I could never do that,"* or, *"I couldn't afford that,"* or, *"Only other people get to do things like that."*

But e*specially* when it comes to coaching, don't let your old programs stop you before you even get started. The fact is, you *could* have a personal coach helping you—and if you can, you *should*. The results of working with a trained coach may seem like magic, but there's no magic to having one.

I've said in these pages that I've spent many years of my life searching for the real solutions to personal growth. In each case, when, after much research, I've found solutions that work, I've presented the best of them to my readers.

This solution, that of having the help of a good coach, is a solution that is without equal. Combined with changing your Self-Talk and learning to set your goals in the right way, having the help of a personal coach will do more to guarantee your ongoing success than any other solution I've ever found.

YOUR TOP SUPPORTER
AND #1 BELIEVER

As I mentioned earlier, although I no longer conduct personal coaching sessions myself, I've become convinced through years of research and studying the results, that _everyone should have a coach._ If we did, we'd all do better. No matter who we are, we can all do better—especially if there is someone helping us and keeping us on the right track.

Every top athlete is coached. In fact, top performers, from athletes to astronauts to business executives, have coaches to keep them focused, on target, and performing at their best. If people who are _already_ top performers need coaches, it would certainly be true for the rest of us. Most of us are not yet at the top of our game—and the right coach could do wonders for _us_.

A good professional coach is your _top supporter, non-critical parent, benevolent teacher, patient listener, trusted friend, tireless motivator_, and _#1 believer_, all rolled into one. Imagine having that kind of person on your side, focusing on who you are and what you want, and helping you get there, every step of the way.

COACHING SOLVES THE BIGGEST PROBLEM OF *SELF*-HELP

There is more to each of us than we will ever realize or experience in our entire lifetime. At our best, we are only seeing a brief flicker of the brilliant light of potential we keep hidden within us. We think we do so much, when at our brightest we are no more than a candle held against the sun.

But even with so much potential within us, and our desire to improve ourselves and reach that potential, the biggest problem with "self-help" is still *self.* It's *us!*

Each of us may have the desire, along with talents and skills and abilities—but all too often those are held back by our own inertia, lack of *direction,* lack of *focus,* lack of *confidence,* lack of *time,* lack of *motivation*—precisely the kinds of challenges a personal coach helps us overcome. Coaching solves the problem; it takes the *self* out of *self*-help.

In many cases, trained coaches are doing more good than a library of self-help books have done in the past; in fact, good coaches bring those great concepts to *life.*

Many people who could have accomplished so much more in their lives have done so little because they haven't been guided or prepared or helped to do any better. (That's where most of us are.) We have the *ability.* We have the *opportunity.* We might even have the *dream.* But *we stay where we are,* living our lives in shades of gray, never experiencing the

189

brilliant light of our own potential—because we don't have the help we need.

Having a coach, on the other hand, gives you that help. Having a coach can translate directly into such things as doing better in your business, having more productive hours in your day, getting more done, getting in control of your weight or taking better care of yourself physically, reaching financial goals, having more spare time to do the things you like, having a better attitude, having less stress, or getting along better with your family.

It is that trained, objective coach who helps you get on track and get moving, and does it in the most down-to-earth and sensible way. A coach doesn't just help you *dream* it. A good coach helps you *reach* it.

A PRACTICAL—BUT *POWERFUL*—PROCESS

How does a personal coach do that? What's the process? What does a personal coach do that somehow magically turns big dreams and small wants into touchable reality? (While goal-setting, as an example, is an "activity" and can be done in solitude, coaching, on the other hand, is an interactive *experience*—it turns *"On"* many more of the chemical switches in the brain—sometimes *all* of them—so the experience itself is not only directly helpful, it's very powerful. Which is why no other personal growth concept quite compares with it.)

190

Yet, note how practical the actual process really is: though different coaches will use a variety of different coaching formats, most coaches accomplish this transformation by holding regular coaching sessions with you, usually once every week or every two weeks.

The coaching sessions are conducted by telephone. Of the various methods of coaching that have been employed, telephone is by far the best. There is an important psychological reason for this. The coaching session is about *you*, and what you want, and how to achieve that. It is *not* about the *coach*. Separated by the telephone distance between you and your coach (who could be across the country), instead of concentrating on the coach, you're focusing on what *counts*. You're not competing with the distractions of an in-person meeting—you're focusing on you.

YOUR TURN TO TALK— YOUR TIME TO *ACHIEVE*

Clients often say that their personal coaching session is the one time during the entire week they look forward to most! That's not surprising. The coaching session itself can be exciting, revealing, revitalizing, *energizing*—and it often is. (Imagine beginning to see a very bright new future being laid out in front of you, week after week, month after month.)

And that's what actually happens. In each session you review your progress for the previous weeks, identify the goal areas you want to focus on for the weeks to come, deal with any problems or obstacles, and decide what action steps you're going to take next. You also discuss key personal growth concepts that will help you move forward in the areas you're working on.

A trained coach knows what to say and what to do next, and most important, your coach knows the right questions to ask. A good coach will not fill the coaching session with his or her opinions or unqualified advice. *It's your turn to talk.* And this time, someone is going to *listen.*

The regular coaching sessions, by themselves, are highly effective for putting you into motion and getting you going in the right direction. But the coaching support goes beyond the coaching session itself. Between sessions it's as though your coach is right there with you as you complete assignments, apply new ideas, track your goals, and work on action steps —motivated by a new level of energy and enthusiasm.

So the benefits you're getting from your coaching, in many ways continue on twenty-four hours a day, seven days a week. The focus, the activity, and the motivation go far beyond the coaching session itself.

With this high level of energy being focused entirely on you and your goals, it could appear at first that you have to set a lot of time aside for the coaching process. But the opposite is true. The coaching process gives you *extra* time. As the coaching helps you set new priorities, organize your time, work smarter, and become more focused and efficient, you end up with more time—less wasted time, and more productive time. So you get more accomplished and have more time for *yourself.*

THE INCREDIBLE POWER OF
COACHING IN ACTION

It's remarkable what happens when you add the concept of coaching to people's lives—and to businesses. Coaching is so effective that it is often a catalyst for almost unbelievable growth and success.

As an example, a friend of mine, Brian Buffini, has become legendary teaching thousands of sales professionals how to build hugely successful businesses, based entirely on "referrals." When he started to train people, Brian had decided to make coaching an integral part of his training and support program for his clients. He combined the best coaching concepts with his unique training program, and offered it to people who were wanting to get ahead in their businesses.

What Brian knew is that when you help people get better, and more in control, in the *other* key areas of their lives—beyond just their businesses—they almost automatically do better in their *businesses* as well.

It worked. Brian's organization, Providence Systems, Inc., now trains and *coaches* thousands of sales professionals each year, and their clients are averaging a *seventy percent increase* in net income the first year they start on the program.

That's remarkable in itself. But you can only imagine the improvements that are taking place in the *other* areas of those clients' lives. My friend Brian now leads the world in teaching professionals how to build their businesses on

193

referrals. But I suspect that through his coaching support, he's *changing* the world in more ways than one.

(If you'd like to get more information on Brian and his program, I've included contact information on the *Resources* page at the end of the book.)

NO MATTER WHERE YOU USE IT, COACHING WORKS

Like my friend, and others in business, or like those who have used coaching in areas such as health and fitness, weight control, recovery, marriage and relationships, building financial strength, and more—we cannot adequately appreciate the value that is gained by making coaching a part of our lives.

The fact is, people who have been coached, or have witnessed coaching for themselves, will tell us that coaching makes *all* the difference.

I'm not surprised. Since its early days, personal coaching in its various forms has grown from being a minor part of self-improvement, to the most important new force in personal growth today. Because of personal coaching, and its accessibility to almost everyone today, life, for many people, *has gotten better*.

One reason coaches are so effective is that they genuinely care about you and helping you succeed. Coaches are real people just like we are—the difference is they've been trained to coach, and the good ones do it well. (I've met a lot of coaches, and without exception, each of them became a coach in the first place because he or she cared about people and wanted to help them do better. I've never found an exception to that.)

Having witnessed the results of personal coaching in people's lives for many years, if you were to ask me today, "What is the *one* thing a person could do to get better, and be almost *certain* of success?" I would answer, "Get a coach."

COACHING CHANGES EVERYTHING

A natural question, then, would be, "How do you find a coach?" or, "How do you become one?"

Not too many years ago there were just a few of these special coaches available, in spite of an increasing demand for their help. Fortunately, today there are a variety of ways to find the right coach or the right coaching program, and it's not difficult to try this exceptional idea for yourself. (I've included sources for information on both finding coaches, and on how to become trained and certified as a life coach, under *Resources* on page 203.)

Professional, personal coaching is one of those few, very special concepts of personal growth that ultimately changes everything. Coaching is already making a profound and positive difference in people's lives, everywhere it touches.

And the story of coaching has just begun.

Chapter Eighteen

Something Wonderful
is Coming

Now it's time to take an exciting step—*up!* To begin, all you have to do is make the choice to take the step. If you do that, and bring together the unfailing support of the three concepts we've discussed here, there's no telling what you can do. But it all begins with your choice to take the step.

To illustrate that first step, imagine that you're standing in the middle of a great field of grain—the kind of field that goes on forever. And in this field, right now, you're standing next to a ladder that goes so far up that it goes into the clouds.

Around you, you see your world—the endless field you're standing in. And in the field there are people just walking around, this way and that, but you can't really tell where they're going, or why.

And then, there's that ladder, out of nowhere, just standing there, in the middle of that endless field.

You look around you and eventually you wonder what you should do next. Field . . . ladder . . . field . . . ladder . . . field . . . ladder . . . and you think, "IImmmm, lct mc scc. Should I do what everyone else I see is doing, and walk around in this field, which is perfectly clear, but doesn't seem to have much in it, or should I take a little risk and step on that first rung of the ladder?"

So you decide, "I think I'll climb up this ladder, because it's the only thing I can see that's not a field." So you start to climb up. First, just one small step. And then, another. And then another. And the higher you go up the ladder, step by step, the farther you can see.

As you climb up, what you see below you is more people walking around in the field. But you keep climbing, and eventually you get high enough up that the field people become indistinct, and start to blur in the distance, and you begin to perceive a whole field of flatness and people who become specks. Which turns into a panorama of sameness. It's a nice field, but it just goes on, without really going anywhere, except more of the same.

But above you is the ladder, reaching up into who knows what? It could go anywhere. And you decide that climbing that ladder, wherever it goes, is *better* than walking around in the field with all those other people who are going who knows where. So you take another step, and then another, and then another.

Somewhere, after taking a lot of steps up, you notice that even people who were close to you at the bottom of the ladder start to lose their definition. They're not all climbing up with you. Some of them look up to see where you're going, but they're afraid to go with you. Some of them may, but some of them will not.

But you can see so much from up here! So you take another step upwards. And then another. You think, "I really want to know where this ladder goes," so you continue.

Then, after a long time of climbing you start to break through—and you climb up through the clouds! And when you do, you can't believe what you find.

Even the air is different! You breathe in a different way. You can feel yourself breathing. The colors are different. More clear. Deep. Intense. The sounds you hear are different; no cacophony of chaos, no dirge of indifference. Up here you hear a peaceful chorus. You can taste the air, and it tastes fresh, and new. When you first started your climb, your hands grasped hard on every rung; some of the steps were even painful to take. But now you seem to float. You hold your hand up, and you can feel the sky.

Here, high up on the ladder, the ceiling of clouds has given way to a beautiful new horizon, and you see the new landscape. Instead of a monotone of endless fields of average, you now see flowers, and parks, and grass, and trees, and running brooks, and butterflies, and swooping swallows. Beautiful swans, in their reflection, mate perfectly with deep, silent water. And everywhere there are footpaths and walkways, and trails. Endless paths that lead to everything imaginable. And on some of those paths you see others who, like you, dared to reach higher. Even up here, beyond the ordinary, you're not alone.

And amongst the beauty of being up here, high above everything down below, in this almost dreamlike garden of endless next steps, you see an amazing thing. You see something that almost no one ever imagines seeing in a park or a garden.

You see more *ladders*! Incredible ladders! Ladders everywhere! All leading *up!* Gold, and silver ladders, and bright and shining ladders, small and grand ladders, leading up from everywhere. Up here there are ladders everywhere! No endless fields of average, like the passive world below. Now you see that everything . . . everything in front of you, no matter how wonderful it is, leads to somewhere *else*—somewhere even better.

And all it took was being willing to take that first step upwards. Out of the day-to-day. Out of the doubt. Out of the negative. Out of the ordinary. And into that incredible world of possibilities . . . that lies just a few steps UP.

TAKE THAT ONE SMALL STEP

In those simple pictures, we see a final truth. The quality of an exceptional life is gained by being willing to seek it. It's not that a better life is impossible to find, but rather that it requires stepping up, above the average, and having the courage to take the next step—and the next.

When we do that, it's not essential that we do it alone. We can even encourage others to go with us—and some of them will. Others will stay where they are. That choice is theirs.

In fact, the most important lesson we can learn about our own personal growth in life, is that the choice to do better, or change, or excel, is up to *each* of us. And it's up to what we choose to do next. So *your* successes, your achievements, your happiness, day after day, will not be up to luck or the winds of chance, or even up to whims of the people around you. Your life, and most of what happens in it, is ultimately up to *you*. How well you do will depend on how much you choose to believe in yourself—and on each next step you take.

That's a truth that tells us so much about the life we have in front of us. It means that success isn't reserved for a chosen few, it is given freely to anyone who chooses it— anyone who is willing to take the next step.

SOMETHING *WONDERFUL* IS COMING

Your choices about what you're going to do next, are up to you. If you begin by making the choice to believe in yourself—no matter *what*—and the choice to take that first step, then there is no limit to what you can do. When I experience the opportunities to take new steps in my own life, I've learned to look forward to them with great and positive anticipation. My own internal Self-Talk gives me the message that says: *"Something wonderful is coming!"*

The same is true for you. Using the tools we've talked about here, the ones that changed my own life—and have helped so many others change theirs—will make that happen for you, too. I encourage you to use these tools for yourself.

Begin by choosing now to get the *best* possible *programs*. Make the "language of success" a part of who you are. Make the new programs and positive messages that the right Self-Talk gives you a part of the background of your everyday life.

While you're doing that, start now to create the habit of *active* goal-setting, and set your *goals* and write them down in the right way—some big goals, and a lot of small ones. Change them when you have to, but read over them every week, stay with them, love working at them, and reach them.

And to tie all of this together—and virtually guarantee your success at whatever you do next—make your first goal to get the help of a good *coach*, and begin to learn what you can do when you have someone else helping you who is completely committed to your success. You'll get focused, you'll stay on track, and you'll have someone supporting and motivating you every step of the way.

If you use these three remarkable concepts *together*—you can be certain that something wonderful *is* coming. With the right *programs*, the right *goals*, and the right *help*, you will open doors to your own future that you might never have known were there, or even thought were open to you.

Many years ago, after taking that same first step, and making that same important choice in my own life, I wrote, as the opening words to my first book:

> *You are everything that is,*
> *your thoughts, your life, your dreams come true.*
> *You are everything you choose to be.*
> *You are as unlimited as the endless universe.*

Those words are true about *you*—right now. That's you!

That's who you really are. *That's* who you were born to *be.* Just think what you can *do,* beginning now. Imagine how far you can go. And it's all up to you—and what you do about it. It's all up to the choices you make, and the next step you take.

It's an exciting thought to know that by taking that small step, by making the choice to truly live up to your best—life for you, once again, is just beginning . . . *and something wonderful is coming.*

Resources

Places to go to get help, information, or materials:

For recorded Self-Talk CDs
www.selftalkstore.com

To print out blank goal-setting forms, or to set goals online
www.goals-on-line.com

To contact or find a life coach
www.findalifecoach.com

For information on training programs to
become a certified life coach
www.lifecoachinstitute.com

For information on business-related coaching, or for information on Brian Buffini and Providence Systems, Inc.
www.findaProCoach.com

For information on coaching and goal-setting
programs for kids and young people
www.goals4kids.com

To subscribe at no charge to Dr. Helmstetter's
E-mail, *"Personal Life Coach Letter"*
www.shadhelmstetter.com

To contact Dr. Helmstetter
shad@shadhelmstetter.com